A SERIES OF JESUS' POWERFUL WORDS

Whoever keeps Jesus' word will never see death.

(John 8, 51)

Book IV

The Teachings of Jesus

Book I: **The Life of Jesus**

Book II: **The Teachings of Jesus About the Trinity**

Book III: **The Parables Told by Jesus**

Book IV: **The Teachings of Jesus**

Book V: **Jesus, the Miracle Maker**

THE TEACHINGS OF JESUS

The teachings of Jesus are the most important teachings for us. Jesus teaches us how to avoid the entanglement of the devil's net and how to refrain from making the wrong decisions

Prepared by
Peter Naumovich, Ph.D.

Grand Island, New York

Address All Inquires to the Publisher:
Naum Publishing
124 Colonial Drive
Grand Island, NY 14072
(716) 240 -7856

Editor: Peter Naumovich, Ph.D.
Technical Editor: Borka Naumovich, M.S.

This volume is published and printed in 2016
Copyright © 2016 by Naum Publishing
NPV19

All rights reserved. No part of this publication may be reproduced, stored in a retrieval system, or transmitted, in any form or by any means, electronic, mechanical, photocopying, recording or otherwise, without the prior permission of Naum Publishing

All excerpts from the Holy Bible, Revised Standard Version, copyrighted © 1995 by the Electronic Text Center University of Virginia, and used with permission

Front cover: Icon of Jesus Christ, Savior and Giver of Life, by Metropolitan Jovan - Zograph, 1393-94, Art Galery, Skopje, Macedonia. Courtesy of the Monastery St. Isaac of Syria Skete, Boscobel, Wisconsin. **Illustrations**: All Illustrations in this book published in the years 1875 through 1910.

Library of Congress Control Number: 2016946509

ISBN 978-0-9830926-3-6

Printed in the United States of America

PREFACE

Our Lord, Jesus Christ, once said: " ... *the word that you hear is not mine, but the Father's who sent me.*" (John 14, 24)

This Bible verse illustrates our only guideline: to compile all the words, thoughts and parables and extract and collect them so that they could be available and useful. All five books contain only verses of the New Testament, because it was only possible way to find these valuable and necessary thoughts and lessons.

Our Lord, Jesus Christ, by executing a task that the Father gave him left us as the most precious treasure of all: the Father's words and thoughts to help us in trouble, until his coming again.

To obtain a true picture of our Savior, his accomplishments and his triumphant resurrection, sometimes it is necessary, apart from the words of Jesus, to cite the thought and words of St. John the Baptist or the apostles. These men were eye-witnesses of the events, all the humiliation and all suffering to which our Savior was exposed, all his short life.

These books consist of all the words, thoughts, sayings and parables of our Lord Himself and they are accepted in all Christian churches.

Archaic Words

art = are

lo = look, see

thee = You
thine = Yours
thou = You
thy = Your

thou didst send = You sent
thou gavest = You have given
thou hast given = You have given
thou hast loved = You have loved
thou hast sent = You have sent
thou shouldst keep = You should keep
thou shouldst take = You should take
thou wilt = You want

CONTENTS AT A GLANCE

ABIDE   1
ABOMINATION   1
ADULTERY   2
AGE   5
ANGRY   5
ANXIOUS   6
ASK   7
AUTHORITY   8

BAPTIZE   10
BEAR FALSE WITNESS   11
BEATING   12
BELIEVE   12
BIRDS   15
BIRTH   16
BLASPHEME   17
BLESSED   17
BLIND   19
BLOOD   19
BOAST   20
BODY   20
BORROW   22
BRANCH   22
BROTHER SINS   23

BURDEN   23

CALLED   24
CARES OF THIS LIFE   24
CARELESS WORD   25
CHILD   26
CHOSEN   27
CHRIST   27
CLOTHING   29
CLOUDS OF HEAVEN   30
COMMANDMENTS   31
COMMUNION   34
CONDEMNED   35
COVERED UP   36
COVETOUSNESS   36
CRITICISM   37

DARKNESS   38
DEATH   39
DECEIT   40
DEMON   41
DENY   43
DEVIL   43
DISHONEST   44
DISSIPATION   44
DIVORCE   44
DOOR (GATE)   46
DOVES   47
DRAW   48
DRUNKENNESS   48

ELECT   49
ENDURANCE   49
ENEMIES   50

ETERNAL LIFE   51
ENVY   57
EUCHARIST   58
EVIL   58
EVIL THINGS   59
EVIL THOUGHTS   40
EXALTED   60
EYE   61

FAITH   62
FAITHFUL   63
FALSE PROPHETS   64
FALSE WITNESS   65
FAST   66
FATHER AND MOTHER   67
FATHER'S WILL   70
FEAR   70
FIG   71
FIRST   72
FLESH   73
FOOD   74
FOOLISHNESS   75
FORGIVE   76
FORNICATION   77
FULL   78

GATE (DOOR)   78
GENTILES   80
GENTLE   81
GIVE   82
GLORY   83
GOD   84
GOD'S WILL   84
GREATEST   85

GUILT   86

HARVEST   86
HATE   87
HEAD OF THE CORNER   90
HEARS   90
HEART OF MAN   90
HIDDEN   94
HOLY   95
HOLY COVENANT   95
HOLY SPIRIT   96, 206
HONOR   97
HUMBLE   98
HUNGER   101
HYPOCRITE   102

JERUSALEM   103
JESUS CHRIST, THE SON OF GOD   105
JUDGMENT   105
JUSTIFIED   108

KILL   109
KINGDOM OF GOD   110
KNOCK   119

LABOR   120
LADEN   120
LAME   120
LAMP   121
LAST   122
LAST DAY   123
LAW   124
LEAVEN   126
LEND   128

LICENTIOUSNESS 128
LIFE 129
LIGHT 132
LOG 135
LORD 136
LORD'S SUPPER 136
LOVE 137
LUSTFULLY 139

MAIMED 140
MAMMON 140
MARRIAGE 141
MASTER 142
MEASURE 143
MEEK 144
MERCYFUL 144
MOTHER AND FATHER 146
MOURN 148
MURDER 149
MUSTARD SEED 150

NEIGHBOR 151

OVERCE 152

PEACEMAKERS 153
PERFECT 153
PERSECUTE 155
PIETY 157
POOR 157
POOR IN SPIRIT 158
POWER 158
POWER OF CHRIST 159
PRAY 162

PRIDE   165
PROCLAIM   166
PROPHETS   167
PURE IN HEART   170

RAISE UP   170
READY   171
REBUKE   172
RECEIVE   172
RECONCILED   172
RENOUNCE   173
REPENT   175
RESIST   177
REST   178
RESURRECTION   178
RESURRECTION OF LIFE   178
RETURN   179
REVEALED   179
REVILE   179
REWARD   180
RICH MAN   181
RIGHTEOUS   182
RULER OF THIS WORLD   185

SABBATH   186
SACRIFICE   187
SALT   188
SATAN   189
SAVED   190
SAVIOR   191
SEEK   192
SERPENTS   193
SERVANT   194
SHEEP   196

Signs 197
Sin 198
Sinners 199
Slander 200
Slave 201
Son of Man 202
Sons of Light 203
Sparrows 203
Speck 204
Spirit 204
Spirit Dumb and Deaf 205
Spirit of God 206
Spirit (Holy Spirit) 206
Steal 207
Swear 208
Sword 208

Tax Collector 209
Teacher 209
Temptation 211
Testimony 212
Theft 212
Thirst 213
Tombs 214
Tradition 214
Treasure 215
Trespasses 215
Tribulation 216
Trouble 216
Truth 217

Unchastity 218

Victor 219

Vine 220

Watch at All Times 220

Wickedness 222
Witness 223
Wolves 224
Word of God 224
Word of Jesus 225
World 226

Yoke 228

If any man would come after me, let him deny himself and take up his cross and follow me. For whoever would save his life will lose it, and whoever loses his life for my sake will find it. (Mt 16, 24. 25)

ABIDE

Abide in Me

Jesus (to his disciples):

bide in me, and I in you. As the branch cannot bear fruit by itself, unless it abides in the vine, neither can you, unless you abide in me.

(John 15, 4)

If You Abide in Me Ask Whatever You Will

Jesus (to his disciples):

f you abide in me, and my words abide in you, ask whatever you will, and it shall be done for you.

(John 15, 7)

ABOMINATION

What Is Exalted Among Men Is an Abomination in the Sight of God

Jesus (to the Pharisees):

ou are those who justify yourselves before men, but God knows your hearts; for what is exalted among men is an abomination in the sight of God.

(Luke 16, 15)

A SERIES OF JESUS' POWERFUL WORDS

ADULTERY

You Shall Not Commit Adultery

Jesus (to the rich young man):

f you would enter life, keep the commandments.

He said to him:

♦ *Which?*

And Jesus said:

You shall not kill, You shall not commit adultery, You shall not steal, You shall not bear false witness, Honor your father and mother, and, You shall love your neighbor as yourself.

The young man said to him:

♦ *All these I have observed; what do I still lack?*

Jesus said to him:

♦ *If you would be perfect, go, sell what you possess and give to the poor, and you will have treasure in heaven; and come, follow me.*

When the young man heard this he went away sorrowful; for he had great possessions.

(Matthew 19, 17 - 22; Mark 10, 19 - 22; Luke 18, 20 - 23)

Whoever Divorces His Wife, Except for Unchastity, Commits Adultery

ow when Jesus had finished these sayings, he went away from Galilee and entered the region of Judea beyond the Jordan; and large crowds followed him, and he healed them there. And Pharisees came up to him and tested him by asking:

♦ *Is it lawful to divorce one's wife for any cause?*

He answered:

♦ *Have you not read that he who made them from the beginning made them male and female, and said, `For this reason a man shall leave his father and mother and be joined to his wife, and the two shall become one flesh'? So they are no longer two but one flesh. What therefore God has joined together, let not man put asunder.*

They said to him:

♦ *Why then did Moses command one to give a certificate of divorce, and to put her away?*

He said to them:

♦ *For your hardness of heart Moses allowed you to divorce your wives, but from the beginning it was not so. And I say to you: whoever divorces his wife, except for unchastity, and marries another, commits adultery.*

The disciples said to him:

♦ *If such is the case of a man with his wife, it is not expedient to marry.*

But he said to them:

♦ *Not all men can receive this saying, but only those to whom it is given. For there are eunuchs who have been so from birth, and there are eunuchs who have been made eunuchs by men, and there are eunuchs who have made themselves eunuchs for the sake of the kingdom of heaven. He who is able to receive this, let him receive it.*

(Matthew 19, 1 - 12; 5, 31. 32; Mark 10, 1 - 12; Luke 16, 18)

Every One Who Looks at a Woman Lustfully Has Already Committed Adultery

(The Sermon on the Mount)

Jesus (to his disciples and the crowds):

ou have heard that it was said, `You shall not commit adultery.' But I say to you that every one who looks at a woman lustfully has already committed adultery with her in his heart.

(Matthew 5, 27. 28)

Out of the Heart of Man, Come Evil Thoughts

nd he (Jesus) called the people to him again, and said to them:

♦ *Hear me, all of you, and understand: there is nothing outside a man which by going into him can defile him; but the things which come out of a man are what defile him.*

And when he had entered the house, and left the people, his disciples asked him about the parable. And he said to them:

♦ *Then are you also without understanding? Do you not see that whatever goes into a man from outside cannot defile him, since it enters, not his heart but his stomach, and so passes on?*

(Thus he declared all foods clean.)

And he said:

♦ *What comes out of a man is what defiles a man. For from within, out of the heart of man, come evil thoughts, fornication, theft, mur-*

der, adultery, coveting, wickedness, deceit, licentiousness, envy, slander, pride, foolishness. All these evil things come from within, and they defile a man.

(Mark 7, 14 - 23;   Matthew 15, 10 - 20)

AGE

I Am with You Always, to the Close of the Age

ow the eleven disciples went to Galilee, to the mountain to which Jesus had directed them. And when they saw him they worshiped him; but some doubted. And Jesus came and said to them:

♦ *All authority in heaven and on earth has been given to me. Go therefore and make disciples of all nations, baptizing them in the name of the Father and of the Son and of the Holy Spirit, teaching them to observe all that I have commanded you; and lo, I am with you always, to the close of the age.*

(Matthew 28, 16 - 20)

ANGRY

Every One Who Is Angry with His Brother Shall Be Liable to Judgment
(The Sermon on the Mount)

Jesus (to his disciples and the crowds):

*ou have heard that it was said to the men of old, `You shall not kill; and whoever kills shall be liable to judgment.' But I say to you that every one who is angry with his brother shall be liable to judgment; whoever insults his brother shall* be liable to the council, and whoever says, `You fool!' shall be liable to the hell of fire.

(Matthew 5, 21. 22)

ANXIOUS

Do Not Be Anxious About Your Life
(The Sermon on the Mount)

Jesus (to his disciples and the crowds):

herefore I tell you, do not be anxious about your life, what you shall eat or what you shall drink, nor about your body, what you shall put on. Is not life more than food, and the body more than clothing?

Look at the birds of the air: they neither sow nor reap nor gather into barns, and yet your heavenly Father feeds them. Are you not of more value than they?

And which of you by being anxious can add one cubit to his span of life?

And why are you anxious about clothing? Consider the lilies of the field, how they grow; they neither toil nor spin; yet I tell you, even Solomon in all his glory was not arrayed like one of these. But if God so clothes the grass of the field, which today is alive and tomorrow is thrown into the oven, will he not much more clothe you, O men of little faith?

Therefore do not be anxious, saying, `What shall we eat?' or ` What shall we drink?' or `What shall we wear?' For the Gentiles seek all these things; and your heavenly Father knows that you need them all. But seek first his kingdom and his righteousness, and all these things shall be yours as well.

Therefore do not be anxious about tomorrow, for tomorrow will be anxious for itself. Let the day's own trouble be sufficient for the day.

(Matthew 6, 25 - 34; Luke 12, 22 - 31)

ASK

Every One Who Asks Receives, and He Who Seeks Finds, and to Him Who Knocks It Will Be Opened

(The Sermon on the Mount)

Jesus (to his disciples and the crowds):

sk, and it will be given you; seek, and you will find; knock, and it will be opened to you. For every one who asks receives, and he who seeks finds, and to him who knocks it will be opened.

Or what man of you, if his son asks him for bread, will give him a stone? Or if he asks for a fish, will give him a serpent? If you then, who are evil, know how to give good gifts to your children, how much more will your Father who is in heaven give good things to those who ask him!

(Matthew 7, 7 - 11; Luke 11, 9 - 13)

If You Ask Anything of the Father, He Will Give It to You in My Name

Jesus (to his disciples):

ruly, truly, I say to you, if you ask anything of the Father, he will give it to you in my name.

(John 16, 23)

A SERIES OF JESUS' POWERFUL WORDS

Whatever You Ask in My Name, I Will Do It

Jesus (to his disciples):

hatever you ask in my name, I will do it, that the Father may be glorified in the Son; if you ask anything in my name, I will do it.

(John 14, 13. 14)

If You Abide in Me Ask Whatever You Will

Jesus (to his disciples):

f you abide in me, and my words abide in you, ask whatever you will, and it shall be done for you. By this my Father is glorified, that you bear much fruit, and so prove to be my disciples.

(John 15, 7. 8)

AUTHORITY

All Authority in Heaven and on Earth Has Been Given to Me

ow the eleven disciples went to Galilee, to the mountain to which Jesus had directed them. And when they saw him they worshiped him; but some doubted. And Jesus came and said to them:

♦ *All authority in heaven and on earth has been given to me. Go therefore and make disciples of all nations, baptizing them in the name of the Father and of the Son and of the Holy Spirit, teaching them to observe all that I have commanded you; and lo, I am with you always, to the close of the age.*

(Matthew 28, 16 - 20)

Power and Authority over All Demons

nd he (Jesus) called the twelve together and gave them power and authority over all demons and to cure diseases, and he sent them out to preach the kingdom of God and to heal. And he said to them:

♦ *Take nothing for your journey, no staff, nor bag, nor bread, nor money; and do not have two tunics. And whatever house you enter, stay there, and from there depart. And wherever they do not receive you, when you leave that town shake off the dust from your feet as a testimony against them.*

And they departed and went through the villages, preaching the gospel and healing everywhere.

(Luke 9, 1 - 6)

For with Authority and Power Jesus Commands the Unclean Spirits?

nd he (Jesus) went down to Capernaum, a city of Galilee. And he was teaching them on the sabbath; and they were astonished at his teaching, for his word was with authority. And in the synagogue there was a man who had the spirit of an unclean demon; and he cried out with a loud voice:

♦ *Ah! What have you to do with us, Jesus of Nazareth? Have you come to destroy us? I know who you are, the Holy One of God.*

But Jesus rebuked him, saying:

♦ *Be silent, and come out of him!*

And when the demon had thrown him down in the midst, he came out of him, having done him no harm. And they were all amazed and said to one another:

♦ *What is this word? For with authority and power he commands the unclean spirits, and they come out.*

And reports of him went out into every place in the surrounding region.

(Luke 4, 31 - 37)

BAPTIZE

He Who Believes and Is Baptized Will Be Saved

Jesus (to his disciples):

e who believes and is baptized will be saved; but he who does not believe will be condemned.

(Mark 16, 16)

Make Disciples of All Nations, Baptizing Them in the Name of the Father and of the Son and of the Holy Spirit

ow the eleven disciples went to Galilee, to the mountain to which Jesus had directed them. And when they saw him they worshiped him; but some doubted. And Jesus came and said to them:

♦ *All authority in heaven and on earth has been given to me. Go therefore and make disciples of all nations, baptizing them in the name of the Father and of the Son and of the Holy Spirit, teaching them to observe all that I have commanded you; and lo, I am with you always, to the close of the age.*

(Matthew 28, 16 - 20)

BEAR FALSE WITNESS
You Shall Not Bear False Witness

Jesus (to the rich young man):

If you would enter life, keep the commandments.

He said to him:

♦ *Which?*

And Jesus said:

You shall not kill, You shall not commit adultery, You shall not steal, You shall not bear false witness, Honor your father and mother, and, You shall love your neighbor as yourself.

The young man said to him:

♦ *All these I have observed; what do I still lack?*

Jesus said to him:

♦ *If you would be perfect, go, sell what you possess and give to the poor, and you will have treasure in heaven; and come, follow me.*

When the young man heard this he went away sorrowful; for he had great possessions.

(Matthew 19, 17 - 22; Mark 10, 19 - 22; Luke 18, 20 - 23)

A SERIES OF JESUS' POWERFUL WORDS

BEATING

A Servant Who Did Not Act According to His Master's Will Would Receive a Severe Beating

Jesus (to his disciples and the crowds):

nd that servant who knew his master's will, but did not make ready or act according to his will, shall receive a severe beating. But he who did not know, and did what deserved a beating, shall receive a light beating. Every one to whom much is given, of him will much be required; and of him to whom men commit much they will demand the more.

(Luke 12, 47. 48)

BELIEVE

Whoever Lives and Believes in Me Shall Never Die

Jesus (to Martha):

am the resurrection and the life; he who believes in me, though he die, yet shall he live, and whoever lives and believes in me shall never die.

(John 11, 25. 26)

All Things Are Possible to Him Who Believes

Jesus (to one of the crowd which son has a dumb spirit):

ow long has he had this?

And he said:

THE TEACHINGS OF JESUS

♦ *From childhood. And it has often cast him into the fire and into the water, to destroy him; but if you can do anything, have pity on us and help us.*

And Jesus said to him:

♦ *If you can! All things are possible to him who believes.*

(Mark 9, 21 - 23)

These Signs Are Written That You May Believe That Jesus Is the Christ, the Son of God

John the Apostle:

 *ow Jesus did many other signs in the presence of the disciples, which are not written in this book; but these are written that you may believe that Jesus is the Christ, the Son of God, and that believing you may have life in his name.*

(John 20, 30. 31)

If My Words Abide in You, Ask Whatever You Will

Jesus (to his disciples):

 *f you abide in me, and my words abide in you, ask whatever you will, and it shall be done for you. By this my Father is glorified, that you bear much fruit, and so prove to be my disciples.*

(John 15, 7. 8)

A SERIES OF JESUS' POWERFUL WORDS

He Who Hears My Word and Believes Him Who Sent Me, Has Eternal Life

Jesus (to the Jews):

ruly, truly, I say to you, he who hears my word and believes him who sent me, has eternal life; he does not come into judgment, but has passed from death to life. Truly, truly, I say to you, the hour is coming, and now is, when the dead will hear the voice of the Son of God, and those who hear will live.

(John 5, 24. 25)

Blessed Are Those Who Have Not Seen and yet Believe

Jesus (to Thomas):

ave you believed because you have seen me? Blessed are those who have not seen and yet believe.

(John 20, 29)

He Who Believes and Is Baptized Will Be Saved

Jesus (to his disciples):

fterward he (Jesus) appeared to the eleven themselves as they sat at table; and he upbraided them for their unbelief and hardness of heart, because they had not believed those who saw him after he had risen. And he said to them:

♦ *Go into all the world and preach the gospel to the whole creation.*

THE TEACHINGS OF JESUS

He who believes and is baptized will be saved; but he who does not believe will be condemned.

(Mark 16, 14 - 16)

I Have Told You Earthly Things and You Do Not Believe

Jesus (to Nicodemus):

f I have told you earthly things and you do not believe, how can you believe if I tell you heavenly things?

(John 3, 12)

BIRDS

Birds Neither Sow Nor Reap Nor Gather into Barns, and yet Your Heavenly Father Feeds Them

(The Sermon on the Mount)

Jesus (to his disciples and the crowds):

herefore I tell you, do not be anxious about your life, what you shall eat or what you shall drink, nor about your body, what you shall put on. Is not life more than food, and the body more than clothing?

Look at the birds of the air: they neither sow nor reap nor gather into barns, and yet your heavenly Father feeds them. Are you not of more value than they?

And which of you by being anxious can add one cubit to his span of life?

And why are you anxious about clothing? Consider the lilies of the field, how they grow; they neither toil nor spin; yet I tell you, even Solomon in all his glory was not arrayed like one of these. But if God so clothes the grass of the field, which today is alive and tomorrow is thrown into the oven, will he not much more clothe you, O men of little faith?

Therefore do not be anxious, saying, `What shall we eat?' or ` What shall we drink?' or `What shall we wear?' For the Gentiles seek all these things; and your heavenly Father knows that you need them all. But seek first his kingdom and his righteousness, and all these things shall be yours as well.

Therefore do not be anxious about tomorrow, for tomorrow will be anxious for itself. Let the day's own trouble be sufficient for the day.

(Matthew 6, 25 - 34;   Luke 12, 22 - 31)

BIRTH

Unless One Is Born of Water and the Spirit, He Cannot Enter the Kingdom of God

Jesus (to Nicodemus):

ruly, truly, I say to you, unless one is born of water and the Spirit, he cannot enter the kingdom of God. That which is born of the flesh is flesh, and that which is born of the Spirit is spirit.

Do not marvel that I said to you, `You must be born anew.' The wind blows where it wills, and you hear the sound of it, but you do not know whence it comes or whither it goes; so it is with every one who is born of the Spirit.

(John 3, 5 - 8)

BLASPHEME

Whoever Blasphemes Against the Holy Spirit Never Has Forgiveness

Jesus (to his disciples and the crowds):

ruly, I say to you, all sins will be forgiven the sons of men, and whatever blasphemies they utter; but whoever blasphemes against the Holy Spirit never has forgiveness, but is guilty of an eternal sin.

(Mark 3, 28. 29)

Whoever Speaks Against the Holy Spirit Will Not Be Forgiven

Jesus (to his disciples and the crowds):

nd whoever says a word against the Son of man will be forgiven; but whoever speaks against the Holy Spirit will not be forgiven, either in this age or in the age to come.

(Matthew 12, 32)

BLESSED

The Beatitudes

(The Sermon on the Mount)

nd great crowds followed him (Jesus) from Galilee and the Decapolis and Jerusalem and Judea and from beyond the Jordan. Seeing the crowds, he went up on the mountain, and when he sat down his disciples came to him. And he opened his mouth and taught them, saying:

♦ *Blessed are the poor in spirit, for theirs is the kingdom of heaven.*

A SERIES OF JESUS' POWERFUL WORDS

Blessed are those who mourn, for they shall be comforted.

Blessed are the meek, for they shall inherit the earth.

Blessed are those who hunger and thirst for righteousness, for they shall be satisfied.

Blessed are the merciful, for they shall obtain mercy.

Blessed are the pure in heart, for they shall see God.

Blessed are the peacemakers, for they shall be called sons of God.

Blessed are those who are persecuted for righteousness' sake, for theirs is the kingdom of heaven.

Blessed are you when men revile you and persecute you and utter all kinds of evil against you falsely on my account.

(Matthew 4, 25; 5, 1 - 11; Luke 6, 17 - 22)

Blessed Are Those Who Have Not Seen and Yet Believe

Jesus (to Thomas):

ave you believed because you have seen me? Blessed are those who have not seen and yet believe.

(John 20, 29)

You Will Be Blessed, Because They Cannot Repay You

ne sabbath when he (Jesus) went to dine at the house of a ruler who belonged to the Pharisees, they were watching him. He said also to the man who had invited him:

♦ *When you give a dinner or a banquet, do not invite your*

THE TEACHINGS OF JESUS

friends or your brothers or your kinsmen or rich neighbors, lest they also invite you in return, and you be repaid. But when you give a feast, invite the poor, the maimed, the lame, the blind, and you will be blessed, because they cannot repay you. You will be repaid at the resurrection of the just.

(Luke 14, 1. 12 - 14)

BLIND

When You Give a Feast, Invite the Poor, the Maimed, the Lame, and the Blind

ne sabbath when he (Jesus) went to dine at the house of a ruler who belonged to the Pharisees, they were watching him. He said also to the man who had invited him:

♦ *When you give a dinner or a banquet, do not invite your friends or your brothers or your kinsmen or rich neighbors, lest they also invite you in return, and you be repaid. But when you give a feast, invite the poor, the maimed, the lame, the blind, and you will be blessed, because they cannot repay you. You will be repaid at the resurrection of the just.*

(Luke 14, 1. 12 - 14)

BLOOD

He Who Eats My Flesh and Drinks My blood I Will Raise Him Up at the Last Day

Jesus (to the Jews):

ruly, truly, I say to you, unless you eat the flesh of the Son of man and drink his blood, you have no life in you; he who eats my flesh and drinks my blood has eternal life, and I

A SERIES OF JESUS' POWERFUL WORDS

will raise him up at the last day. For my flesh is foo indeed, and my blood is drink indeed.

(John 6, 53 - 55)

BOAST

I Will All the More Gladly Boast of My Weaknesses

Paul (to Corinthians):

nd to keep me from being too elated by the abundance of revelations, a thorn was given me in the flesh, a messenger of Satan, to harass me, to keep me from being too elated. Three times I besought the Lord about this, that it should leave me; but he said to me:

➢ *My grace is sufficient for you, for my power is made perfect in weakness.*

I will all the more gladly boast of my weaknesses, that the power of Christ may rest upon me.

(2. Corinthians 12, 7 - 9)

BODY

Is Not Life More Than Food, and the Body More Than Clothing?
(The Sermon on the Mount)

Jesus (to his disciples and the crowds):

herefore I tell you, do not be anxious about your life, what you shall eat or what you shall drink, nor about your body, what you shall put on. Is not life more than food, and the

body more than clothing?

Look at the birds of the air: they neither sow nor reap nor gather into barns, and yet your heavenly Father feeds them. Are you not of more value than they?

And which of you by being anxious can add one cubit to his span of life?

And why are you anxious about clothing?

Consider the lilies of the field, how they grow; they neither toil nor spin; yet I tell you, even Solomon in all his glory was not arrayed like one of these.

But if God so clothes the grass of the field, which today is alive and tomorrow is thrown into the oven, will he not much more clothe you, O men of little faith?

Therefore do not be anxious, saying, `What shall we eat?' or ` What shall we drink?' or `What shall we wear?' For the Gentiles seek all these things; and your heavenly Father knows that you need them all.

But seek first his kingdom and his righteousness, and all these things shall be yours as well.

Therefore do not be anxious about tomorrow, for tomorrow will be anxious for itself.

Let the day's own trouble be sufficient for the day.

(Matthew 6, 25 - 34; Luke 12, 22 - 31)

A SERIES OF JESUS' POWERFUL WORDS

BORROW

Do Not Refuse Him Who Would Borrow from You

(The Sermon on the Mount)

Jesus (to his disciples and the crowds):

ive to him who begs from you, and do not refuse him who would borrow from you.

(Matthew 5, 42; Luke 6, 30)

BRANCH

As the Branch Cannot Bear Fruit by Itself, Apart from Me You Can Do Nothing

Jesus (to his disciples):

bide in me, and I in you.

As the branch cannot bear fruit by itself, unless it abides in the vine, neither can you, unless you abide in me.

I am the vine, you are the branches.

He who abides in me, and I in him, he it is that bears much fruit, for apart from me you can do nothing.

If a man does not abide in me, he is cast forth as a branch and withers; and the branches are gathered, thrown into the fire and burned.

If you abide in me, and my words abide in you, ask whatever you will, and it shall be done for you.

By this my Father is glorified, that you bear much fruit, and so prove to be my disciples.

(John 15, 4 - 6)

BROTHER'S SIN

If Your Brother Sins Against You, Go and Tell Him

Jesus (to his disciples):

f your brother sins against you, go and tell him his fault, between you and him alone. If he listens to you, you have gained your brother. But if he does not listen, take one or two others along with you, that every word may be confirmed by the evidence of two or three witnesses.

If he refuses to listen to them, tell it to the church; and if he refuses to listen even to the church, let him be to you as a Gentile and a tax collector.

(Matthew 18, 15 - 17)

BURDEN

My Yoke Is Easy, and My Burden Is Light

Jesus (to his disciples and the crowds):

ome to me, all who labor and are heavy laden, and I will give you rest. Take my yoke upon you, and learn from me; for I am gentle and lowly in heart, and you will find rest for your souls. For my yoke is easy, and my burden is light.

(Matthew 11, 28 - 30)

CALLED

Many Are Called

Jesus (to the chief Priests and the Pharisees):

any are called, but few are chosen.

(Matthew 22, 14; Luke 14, 24)

CARES OF THIS LIFE

Take Heed to Yourselves Lest Your Hearts Be Weighed Down with Cares of This Life

Jesus (to his disciples):

ut take heed to yourselves lest your hearts be weighed down with dissipation and drunkenness and cares of this life, and that day come upon you suddenly like a snare; for it will come upon all who dwell upon the face of the whole earth.

But watch at all times, praying that you may have strength to escape all these things that will take place, and to stand before the Son of man.

(Luke 21, 34 - 36; Matthew 24, 42; 25, 13; Mark 13, 33)

Do Not Be Anxious About Tomorrow
(The Sermon on the Mount)

Jesus (to his disciples and the crowds):

herefore I tell you, do not be anxious about your life, what you shall eat or what you shall drink, nor about your body, what you shall put on. Is not life more than food, and the body more than clothing?

Look at the birds of the air: they neither sow nor reap nor gather into barns, and yet your heavenly Father feeds them. Are you not of more value than they?

And which of you by being anxious can add one cubit to his span of life?

And why are you anxious about clothing? Consider the lilies of the field, how they grow; they neither toil nor spin; yet I tell you, even Solomon in all his glory was not arrayed like one of these. But if God so clothes the grass of the field, which today is alive and tomorrow is thrown into the oven, will he not much more clothe you, O men of little faith?

Therefore do not be anxious, saying, `What shall we eat?' or ` What shall we drink?' or `What shall we wear?' For the Gentiles seek all these things; and your heavenly Father knows that you need them all. But seek first his kingdom and his righteousness, and all these things shall be yours as well. Therefore do not be anxious about tomorrow, for tomorrow will be anxious for itself. Let the day's own trouble be sufficient for the day.

(Matthew 6, 25 - 34; Luke 12, 22 - 31)

CARELESS WORD

On The Day of Judgment Men Will Render Account for Every Careless Word They Utter

Jesus (to the Pharisees):

tell you, on the day of judgment men will render account for every careless word they utter; for by your words you will be justified, and by your words you will be condemned.

(Matthew 12, 36. 37)

CHILD

Humble Himself Like a Child

At that time the disciples came to Jesus, saying:

♦ *Who is the greatest in the kingdom of heaven?*

And calling to him a child, he put him in the midst of them, and said:

♦ *Truly, I say to you, unless you turn and become like children, you will never enter the kingdom of heaven.*

Whoever humbles himself like this child, he is the greatest in the kingdom of heaven.

Whoever receives one such child in my name receives me; but whoever causes one of these little ones who believe in me to sin, it would be better for him to have a great millstone fastened round his neck and to be drowned in the depth of the sea.

(Matthew 18, 1 - 6; Mark 9, 35 - 37; Luke 9, 46 - 48)

Their Angels Always Behold the Face of My Father

Jesus (to his disciples):

See that you do not despise one of these little ones; for I tell you that in heaven their angels always behold the face of my Father who is in heaven. So it is not the will of my Father who is in heaven that one of these little ones should perish.

(Matthew 18, 10. 14)

Receive the Kingdom of God Like a Child

nd they (his disciples) were bringing children to him (Jesus), that he might touch them; and the disciples rebuked them. But when Jesus saw it he was indignant, and said to them:

♦ *Let the children come to me, do not hinder them; for to such belongs the kingdom of God. Truly, I say to you, whoever does not receive the kingdom of God like a child shall not enter it.*

And he took them in his arms and blessed them, laying his hands upon them.

(Mark 10, 13 - 16; Matthew 19, 13. 14; 18, 3; Luke 18, 15 - 17)

CHOSEN

Few Are Chosen

Jesus (to the chief Priests and the Pharisees):

any are called, but few are chosen.

(Matthew 22, 14; Luke 14, 24)

CHRIST

Whose Son Is the Christ?

ow while the Pharisees were gathered together, Jesus asked them a question, saying:

♦ *What do you think of the Christ? Whose son is he?*

They said to him:

A SERIES OF JESUS' POWERFUL WORDS

♦ *The son of David.*

He said to them:

♦ *How is it then that David, inspired by the Spirit, calls him Lord, saying, 'The Lord said to my Lord, Sit at my right hand, till I put thy enemies under thy feet'? If David thus calls him Lord, how is he his son?*

And no one was able to answer him a word, nor from that day did any one dare to ask him any more questions.

(Matthew 22, 41 - 46)

If any Man Would Come After Me, Let Him Deny Himself and Take Up His Cross and Follow Me

Jesus (to his disciples):

f any man would come after me, let him deny himself and take up his cross and follow me. For whoever would save his life will lose it, and whoever loses his life for my sake will find it.

(Matthew 16, 24. 25; 10, 38. 39; Mark 8, 34. 35; Luke 9, 23. 24; 17, 33; John 12, 25)

You Are the Christ, the Son of the Living God

ow when Jesus came into the district of Caesarea Philippi, he asked his disciples:

♦ *Who do men say that the Son of man is?*

And they said:

- *Some say John the Baptist, others say Elijah, and others Jeremiah or one of the prophets.*

He said to them:

- *But who do you say that I am?*

Simon Peter replied:

- *You are the Christ, the Son of the living God.*

And Jesus answered him:

- *Blessed are you, Simon Bar-Jona! For flesh and blood has not revealed this to you, but my Father who is in heaven.*

(Matthew 16, 13 - 17)

CLOTHING

Is Not Life More Than Food, and The Body More Than Clothing?

(The Sermon on the Mount)

Jesus (to his disciples and the crowds):

herefore I tell you, do not be anxious about your life, what you shall eat or what you shall drink, nor about your body, what you shall put on. Is not life more than food, and the body more than clothing?

Look at the birds of the air: they neither sow nor reap nor gather into barns, and yet your heavenly Father feeds them. Are you not of more value than they?

And which of you by being anxious can add one cubit to his span of life?

And why are you anxious about clothing? Consider the lilies of the field, how they grow; they neither toil nor spin; yet I tell you, even Solomon in all his glory was not arrayed like one of these. But if God so clothes the grass of the field, which today is alive and tomorrow is thrown into the oven, will he not much more clothe you, O men of little faith?

Therefore do not be anxious, saying, `What shall we eat?' or ` What shall we drink?' or `What shall we wear?' For the Gentiles seek all these things; and your heavenly Father knows that you need them all. But seek first his kingdom and his righteousness, and all these things shall be yours as well.

Therefore do not be anxious about tomorrow, for tomorrow will be anxious for itself. Let the day's own trouble be sufficient for the day.

(Matthew 6, 25 - 34; Luke 12, 22 - 31)

CLOUDS OF HEAVEN

You Will See the Son of Man Seated at the Right Hand of Power, and Coming on the Clouds of Heaven

ut Jesus was silent. And the high priest said to him:

♦ *I adjure you by the living God, tell us if you are the Christ, the Son of God.*

Jesus said to him:

♦ *You have said so. But I tell you, hereafter you will see the Son of man seated at the right hand of Power, and coming on the clouds of heaven.*

(Matthew 26, 63. 64, Luke 22, 67 - 69)

COMMANDMENTS

About Commandments
(The Sermon on the Mount)

Jesus (to his disciples and the crowds):

hink not that I have come to abolish the law and the prophets; I have come not to abolish them but to fulfil them. For truly, I say to you, till heaven and earth pass away, not an iota, not a dot, will pass from the law until all is accomplished. Whoever then relaxes one of the least of these commandments and teaches men so, shall be called least in the kingdom of heaven; but he who does them and teaches them shall be called great in the kingdom of heaven.

(Matthew 5, 17 - 19)

Which Commandment Is the First of All?

nd one of the scribes came up and heard them disputing with one another, and seeing that he answered them well, asked him:

♦ *Which commandment is the first of all?*

Jesus answered:

♦ *The first is, `Hear, O Israel: The Lord our God, the Lord is one; and you shall love the Lord your God with all your heart, and with all your soul, and with all your mind, and with all your strength.' The second is this, `You shall love your neighbor as yourself.' There is no other commandment greater than these.*

And the scribe said to him:

♦ *You are right, Teacher; you have truly said that he is one, and there is no other but he; and to love him with all the heart, and with all the understanding, and with all the strength, and to love one's neighbor as oneself, is much more than all whole burnt offerings and sacrifices.*

And when Jesus saw that he answered wisely, he said to him:

♦ *You are not far from the kingdom of God.*

And after that no one dared to ask him any question.

(Mark 12, 28 - 34; Matthew 22, 34 - 40; Luke 10, 25 - 28)

If You Would Enter Life, Keep the Commandments

nd behold, one came up to him (Jesus) , saying:

♦ *Teacher, what good deed must I do, to have eternal life?*

And he said to him:

♦ *Why do you ask me about what is good? One there is who is good. If you would enter life, keep the commandments.*

He said to him:

♦ *Which?*

And Jesus said:

♦ *You shall not kill, You shall not commit adultery, You shall not steal, You shall not bear false witness, Honor your father and mother, and, You shall love your neighbor as yourself.*

The young man said to him:

♦ *All these I have observed; what do I still lack?*

Jesus said to him:

♦ *If you would be perfect, go, sell what you possess and give to the poor, and you will have treasure in heaven; and come, follow me.*

When the young man heard this he went away sorrowful; for he had great possessions.

(Matthew 19, 16 - 22; Mark 10, 19 - 22; Luke 18, 20 - 23)

If You Keep My Commandments, You Will Abide in My Love

Jesus (to his disciples):

ف you keep my commandments, you will abide in my love, just as I have kept my Father's commandments and abide in his love. These things I have spoken to you, that my joy may be in you, and that your joy may be full.

(John 15, 10. 11)

A New Commandment I Give to You, That You Love One Another

Jesus (to his disciples):

new commandment I give to you, that you love one another; even as I have loved you, that you also love one another. By this all men will know that you are my disciples, if you have love for one another.

(John 13, 34. 35)

You Are My Friends if You Do What I Command You

Jesus (to his disciples):

reater love has no man than this, that a man lay down his life for his friends. You are my friends if you do what I command you.

(John 15, 13. 14)

He Who Has My Commandments and Keeps Them, Is He Who Loves Me

Jesus (to his disciples):

e who has my commandments and keeps them, he it is who loves me; and he who loves me will be loved by my Father, and I will love him and manifest myself to him.

(John 14, 21)

COMMUNION

This Is My Blood of the Covenant, Which Is Poured Out for Many for the Forgiveness of Sins

ow as they were eating, Jesus took bread, and blessed, and broke it, and gave it to the disciples and said:

♦ *Take, eat; this is my body.*

And he took a cup, and when he had given thanks he gave it to them, saying:

♦ *Drink of it, all of you; for this is my blood of the covenant, which is poured out for many for the forgiveness of sins. I tell you I shall not drink again of this fruit of the vine until that day when I drink it new with you in my Father's kingdom.*

And when they had sung a hymn, they went out to the Mount of Olives.

(Matthew 26, 26 - 30; Mark 14, 22 - 27; Luke 22, 14 - 20)

CONDEMNED

He Who Does Not Believe Will Be Condemned

Jesus (to his disciples):

e who believes and is baptized will be saved; but he who does not believe will be condemned.

(Mark 16, 16)

By Your Words You Will Be Condemned

Jesus (to the Pharisees):

tell you, on the day of judgment men will render account for every careless word they utter; for by your words you will be justified, and by your words you will be condemned.

(Matthew 12, 36. 37)

A SERIES OF JESUS' POWERFUL WORDS

COVERED UP

Nothing Is Covered Up That Will Not Be Revealed

n the meantime, when so many thousands of the multitude had gathered together that they trod upon one another, he (Jesus) began to say to his disciples first:

♦ *Beware of the leaven of the Pharisees, which is hypocrisy. Nothing is covered up that will not be revealed, or hidden that will not be known. Therefore whatever you have said in the dark shall be heard in the light, and what you have whispered in private rooms shall be proclaimed upon the housetops.*

(Luke 12, 1 - 3)

COVETOUSNESS

Out of the Heart of Man, Come Evil Thoughts,

nd he (Jesus) called the people to him again, and said to them:

♦ *Hear me, all of you, and understand: there is nothing outside a man which by going into him can defile him; but the things which come out of a man are what defile him.*

And when he had entered the house, and left the people, his disciples asked him about the parable. And he said to them:

♦ *Then are you also without understanding? Do you not see that whatever goes into a man from outside cannot defile him, since it enters, not his heart but his stomach, and so passes on?*

(Thus he declared all foods clean.)

And he said:

♦ *What comes out of a man is what defiles a man. For from within, out of the heart of man, come evil thoughts, fornication, theft, murder, adultery, coveting, wickedness, deceit, licentiousness, envy, slander, pride, foolishness. All these evil things come from within, and they defile a man.*

(Mark 7, 14 - 23; Matthew 15, 10 - 20)

Beware of All Covetousness

ne of the multitude said to him (Jesus):

♦ *Teacher, bid my brother divide the inheritance with me.*

But he said to him:

♦ *Man, who made me a judge or divider over you?*

And he said to them:

♦ *Take heed, and beware of all covetousness; for a man's life does not consist in the abundance of his possessions.*

(Luke 12, 13 - 15)

CRITICISM

Judge Not, That You Be Not Judged
(The Sermon on the Mount)

Jesus (to his disciples and the crowds):

*udge not, that you be not judged. For with the judgment you pronounce you will be judged, and the measure you give will be the measure you get.*

(Matthew 7, 1. 2; Luke 6, 37)

The Measure You Give Will Be the Measure You Get

Jesus (to his disciples):

ake heed what you hear; the measure you give will be the measure you get, and still more will be given you. For to him who has will more be given; and from him who has not, even what he has will be taken away.

(Mark 4, 24. 25; Luke 8, 18)

DARKNESS

Who Walks in the Darkness Does Not Know Where He Goes

Jesus (to his disciples and the crowds):

he light is with you for a little longer. Wake while you have the light, lest the darkness overtake you; he who wakes in the darkness does not know where he goes. While you have the light, believe in the light, that you may become sons of light.

(John 12, 35. 36)

When Your Eye Is Not Sound, Your Body Is Full of Darkness

Jesus (to his disciples and the crowds):

our eye is the lamp of your body; when your eye is sound, your whole body is full of light; but when it is not sound, your body is full of darkness. Therefore be careful lest the light in you be darkness. If then your whole body is full of

THE TEACHINGS OF JESUS

light, having no part dark, it will be wholly bright, as when a lamp with its rays gives you light.

(Luke 11, 34 - 36)

♦ *If your eye is not sound, your whole body will be full of darkness. If then the light in you is darkness, how great is the darkness!*

(Matthew 6, 23)

DEATH

Whoever Lives and Believes in Me Shall Never Die

Jesus (to Martha):

am the resurrection and the life; he who believes in me, though he die, yet shall he live, and whoever lives and believes in me shall never die.

(John 11, 25. 26)

He Who Hears My Word and Believes Him Who Sent Me, Has Passed from Death to Life

Jesus (to the Jews):

ruly, truly, I say to you, he who hears my word and believes him who sent me, has eternal life; he does not come into judgment, but has passed from death to life.

Truly, truly, I say to you, the hour is coming, and now is, when the dead will hear the voice of the Son of God, and those who hear will live.

For as the Father has life in himself, so he has granted the Son

A SERIES OF JESUS' POWERFUL WORDS

also to have life in himself, and has given him authority to execute judgment, because he is the Son of man.

Do not marvel at this; for the hour is coming when all who are in the tombs will hear his voice and come forth, those who have done good, to the resurrection of life, and those who have done evil, to the resurrection of judgment.

(John 5, 24 - 29)

There Are Some Standing Here Who Will Not Taste Death

Jesus (to his disciples):

ruly, I say to you, there are some standing here who will not taste death before they see the Son of man coming in his kingdom.

(Matthew 16, 28; Mark 9, 1; Luke 9, 27)

DECEIT

Out of the Heart of Man, Come Evil Thoughts

nd he (Jesus) called the people to him again, and said to them:

♦ *Hear me, all of you, and understand: there is nothing outside a man which by going into him can defile him; but the things which come out of a man are what defile him.*

And when he had entered the house, and left the people, his disciples asked him about the parable. And he said to them:

♦ *Then are you also without understanding? Do you not see that whatever goes into a man from outside cannot defile him, since it enters, not his heart but his stomach, and so passes on?*

(Thus he declared all foods clean.)

And he said:

♦ *What comes out of a man is what defiles a man. For from within, out of the heart of man, come evil thoughts, fornication, theft, murder, adultery, coveting, wickedness, deceit, licentiousness, envy, slander, pride, foolishness. All these evil things come from within, and they defile a man.*

(Mark 7, 14 - 23;   Matthew 15, 10 - 20)

DEMONS

Jesus Casts Out Demons by the Spirit of God

Jesus (to the Pharisees):

ut *if it is by the Spirit of God that I cast out demons, then the kingdom of God has come upon you.*

(Matthew 12, 28; Luke 11, 20)

With Faith the Size of a Mustard Seed

hen the disciples came to Jesus privately and said:

♦ *Why could we not cast it out?*

He said to them:

♦ *Because of your little faith. For truly, I say to you, if you have faith*

A SERIES OF JESUS' POWERFUL WORDS

as a grain of mustard seed, you will say to this mountain, 'Move from here to there,' and it will move; and nothing will be impossible to you.

(Matthew 17, 19. 20)

Jesus Casts Out Demons by the Spirit of God

Jesus (to the Pharisees):

ut if it is by the Spirit of God that I cast out demons, then the kingdom of God has come upon you.

(Matthew 12, 28; Luke 11, 20)

This Kind Cannot Be Driven Out by Anything but Prayer

nd when he (Jesus) had entered the house, his disciples asked him privately:

♦ *Why could we not cast it out?*

And he said to them:

♦ *This kind cannot be driven out by anything but prayer.*

(Mark 9, 28. 29)

In My Name They Will Cast Out Demons

Jesus (to the eleven):

o into all the world and preach the gospel to the whole creation. He who believes and is baptized will be saved; but he who does not believe will be condemned. And these signs will accompany those who believe: in my name they will cast out demons; they will speak in new tongues; they will pick up serpents, and if they drink any deadly thing, it will not hurt them; they will lay their hands on the sick, and they will recover.

(Mark 16, 15 - 18; Luke 10, 19)

DENY

If Any Man Would Come After Me, Let Him Deny Himself and Take Up His Cross and Follow Me

Jesus (to his disciples):

f any man would come after me, let him deny himself and take up his cross and follow me. For whoever would save his life will lose it, and whoever loses his life for my sake will find it. For what will it profit a man, if he gains the whole world and forfeits his life? Or what shall a man give in return for his life?

(Matthew 16, 24 - 26; 10, 38. 39; Mark 8, 34. 35; Luke 9, 23. 24; 17, 33; John 12, 25)

DEVIL

The Devil Is a Liar and the Father of Lies

Jesus (to the Jews):

hy do you not understand what I say? It is because you cannot bear to hear my word. You are of your father the devil, and your will is to do your father's desires. He was a murderer from the beginning, and has nothing to do with the truth, because there is no truth in him. When he lies, he speaks according to his own nature, for he is a liar and the father of lies.

(John 8, 43. 44)

DISHONEST

He Who Is Dishonest in a Very Little
Is Dishonest Also in Much

Jesus (to his disciples):

e who is faithful in a very little is faithful also in much; and he who is dishonest in a very little is dishonest also in much.

(Luke 16, 10; 19, 17; Matthew 25, 21)

DISSIPATION

Take Heed to Yourselves Lest Your Hearts
Be Weighed Down with Dissipation

Jesus (to his disciples):

ut take heed to yourselves lest your hearts be weighed down with dissipation and drunkenness and cares of this life, and that day come upon you suddenly like a snare; for it will come upon all who dwell upon the face of the whole earth. But watch at all times, praying that you may have strength to escape all these things that will take place, and to stand before the Son of man.

(Luke 21, 34 - 36; Matthew 24, 42; 25, 13; Mark 13, 33)

DIVORCE

What Therefore God Has Joined Together,
Let Not Man Put Asunder

ow when Jesus had finished these sayings, he went away from Galilee and entered the region of Judea beyond the Jordan; and large crowds followed him, and he healed them there. And Pharisees came up to him and tested him by asking:

♦ *Is it lawful to divorce one's wife for any cause?*

He answered:

♦ *Have you not read that he who made them from the beginning made them male and female, and said, 'For this reason a man shall leave his father and mother and be joined to his wife, and the two shall become one flesh'? So they are no longer two but one flesh. What therefore God has joined together, let not man put asunder.*

They said to him:

♦ *Why then did Moses command one to give a certificate of divorce, and to put her away?*

He said to them:

♦ *For your hardness of heart Moses allowed you to divorce your wives, but from the beginning it was not so. And I say to you: whoever divorces his wife, except for unchastity, and marries another, commits adultery.*

The disciples said to him:

♦ *If such is the case of a man with his wife, it is not expedient to marry.*

But he said to them:

♦ *Not all men can receive this saying, but only those to whom it is given. For there are eunuchs who have been so from birth, and there are eunuchs who have been made eunuchs by men, and there are eunuchs who have made themselves eunuchs for the sake of the kingdom of heaven. He who is able to receive this, let him receive it.*

(Matthew 19, 1 - 12; 5, 31. 32; Mark 10, 1 - 12; Luke 16, 18)

DOOR (GATE)

Enter by the Narrow Gate
(The Sermon on the Mount)

Jesus (to his disciples and the crowds):

nter by the narrow gate; for the gate is wide and the way is easy, that leads to destruction, and those who enter by it are many. For the gate is narrow and the way is hard, that leads to life, and those who find it are few.

(Matthew 7, 13. 14; Luke 13, 24)

Strive to Enter by the Narrow Door

e (Jesus) went on his way through towns and villages, teaching, and journeying toward Jerusalem. And some one said to him:

♦ *Lord, will those who are saved be few?*

And he said to them:

♦ *Strive to enter by the narrow door; for many, I tell you, will seek to enter and will not be able.*

When once the householder has risen up and shut the door, you will begin to stand outside and to knock at the door, saying, `Lord, open to us.' He will answer you, `I do not know where you come from.' Then you will begin to say, `We ate and drank in your presence, and* *you taught in our streets.' But he will say, `I tell you, I do not know where you come from; depart from me, all you workers of iniquity!' There you will weep and gnash your teeth, when you see Abraham and Isaac and Jacob and all the prophets in the kingdom of God and you yourselves thrust out.

And men will come from east and west, and from north and south, and sit at table in the kingdom of God. And behold, some are last who will be first, and some are first who will be last.

(Luke 13, 22 - 30)

DOVES

Be Wise As Serpents and Innocent As Doves

Jesus (to his disciples):

ehold, I send you out as sheep in the midst of wolves; so be wise as serpents and innocent as doves. Beware of men; for they will deliver you up to councils, and flog you in their synagogues, and you will be dragged before governors and kings for my sake, to bear testimony before them and the Gentiles. When they deliver you up, do not be anxious how you are to speak or what you are to say; for what you are to say will be given to you in that hour; for it is not you who speak, but the Spirit of your Father speaking through you.

(Matthew 10, 16 - 20; Luke 10, 3)

A SERIES OF JESUS' POWERFUL WORDS

DRAW

No One Can Come to Me Unless the Father Draws Him

Jesus (to the Jews):

o one can come to me unless the Father who sent me draws him; and I will raise him up at the last day.

It is written in the prophets, 'And they shall all be taught by God.' Every one who has heard and learned from the Father comes to me.

Not that any one has seen the Father except him who is from God; he has seen the Father.

(John 6, 44 - 46)

DRUNKENNESS

Take Heed to Yourselves, Lest Your Hearts Be Weighed Down with Drunkenness

Jesus (to his disciples):

ut take heed to yourselves lest your hearts be weighed down with dissipation and drunkenness and cares of this life, and that day come upon you suddenly like a snare; for it will come upon all who dwell upon the face of the whole earth.

But watch at all times, praying that you may have strength to escape all these things that will take place, and to stand before the Son of man.

(Luke 21, 34 - 36; Matthew 24, 42; 25, 13; Mark 13, 33)

ELECT

His Angels Will Gather His Elect from the Four Winds, from One End of Heaven to the Other

Jesus (to his disciples):

or as the lightning comes from the east and shines as far as the west, so will be the coming of the Son of man. Wherever the body is, there the eagles will be gathered together.

Immediately after the tribulation of those days the sun will be darkened, and the moon will not give its light, and the stars will fall from heaven, and the powers of the heavens will be shaken; then will appear the sign of the Son of man in heaven, and then all the tribes of the earth will mourn, and they will see the Son of man coming on the clouds of heaven with power and great glory; and he will send out his angels with a loud trumpet call, and they will gather his elect from the four winds, from one end of heaven to the other.

From the fig tree learn its lesson: as soon as its branch becomes tender and puts forth its leaves, you know that summer is near. So also, when you see all these things, you know that he is near, at the very gates.

(Matthew 24, 27 - 33; Mark 13, 24 - 29)

ENDURANCE

Gaining Your Lives

Jesus (to his disciples):

y your endurance you will gain your lives.

(Luke 21, 19; Matthew 24, 13)

ENEMIES

Love Your Enemies
(The Sermon on the Mount)

Jesus (to his disciples and the crowds):

ou have heard that it was said, `You shall love your neighbor and hate your enemy.' But I say to you, Love your enemies and pray for those who persecute you, so that you may be sons of your Father who is in heaven; for he makes his sun rise on the evil and on the good, and sends rain on the just and on the unjust.

For if you love those who love you, what reward have you? Do not even the tax collectors do the same?

And if you salute only your brethren, what more are you doing than others? Do not even the Gentiles do the same?

You, therefore, must be perfect, as your heavenly Father is perfect.

(Matthew 5, 43 - 48; Luke 6, 27. 28. 32. 35. 36)

Love Your Enemies, Do Good, and Lend, Expecting Nothing in Return
(The Sermon on the Mount)

Jesus (to his disciples and a great multitude
    of people from all Judea and Jerusalem
    and the seacost of Tyre and Sidon):

nd as you wish that men would do to you, do so to them. If you love those who love you, what credit is that to you? For even sinners love those who love them. And if you do good to those who do good to you, what credit is that to you?

For even sinners do the same. And if you lend to those from whom you hope to receive, what credit is that to you? Even sinners lend to sinners, to receive as much again.

But love your enemies, and do good, and lend, expecting nothing in return; and your reward will be great, and you will be sons of the Most High; for he is kind to the ungrateful and the selfish. Be merciful, even as your Father is merciful.

(Luke 6, 31 - 36, Matthew 5, 43 – 48)

ETERNAL LIFE

He Who Eats My Flesh and Drinks My Blood Has Eternal Life

Jesus (to the Jews):

ruly, truly, I say to you, unless you eat the flesh of the Son of man and drink his blood, you have no life in you; he who eats my flesh and drinks my blood has eternal life, and I will raise him up at the last day. For my flesh is foo indeed, and my blood is drink indeed.

(John 6, 53 - 55)

He Who Hears My Word and Believes Him Who Sent Me, Has Eternal Life

Jesus (to the Jews):

ruly, truly, I say to you, he who hears my word and believes him who sent me, has eternal life; he does not come into judgment, but has passed from death to life.

(John 5, 24)

A SERIES OF JESUS' POWERFUL WORDS

He Who Hates His Life in This World Will Keep It for Eternal Life

Jesus (to his disciples):

e who loves his life loses it, and he who hates his life in this world will keep it for eternal life.

(John 12, 25)

How to Inherit Eternal Life

Jesus (to his disciples):

nd every one who has left houses or brothers or sisters or father or mother or children or lands, for my name's sake, will receive a hundredfold, and inherit eternal life. But many that are first will be last, and the last first.

(Matthew 19, 29. 30;   Mark 10, 28 - 31;   Luke 18, 28 -30)

If You Would Enter Life, Keep the Commandments

Jesus (to the rich young man):

f you would enter life, keep the commandments.

He said to him:

♦ *Which?*

And Jesus said:

You shall not kill, You shall not commit adultery, You shall not steal, You shall not bear false witness, Honor your father and mother, and, You shall love your neighbor as yourself.

THE TEACHINGS OF JESUS

The young man said to him:

♦ *All these I have observed; what do I still lack?*

Jesus said to him:

♦ *If you would be perfect, go, sell what you possess and give to the poor, and you will have treasure in heaven; and come, follow me.*

When the young man heard this he went away sorrowful; for he had great possessions.

(Matthew 19, 17 - 22; Mark 10, 19 - 22; Luke 18, 20 - 23)

This Is Eternal Life, That They Know Thee, the Only True God and Jesus Christ Whom Thou Hast Sent

Jesus lifted up his eyes to heaven and said:

ather, the hour has come; glorify thy Son that the Son may glorify thee, since thou hast given him power over all flesh, to give eternal life to all whom thou hast given him. And this is eternal life, that they know thee the only true God, and Jesus Christ whom thou hast sent.

(John 17, 1 - 3)

I Know That His Commandment Is Eternal Life

Jesus (to his disciples and the crowds):

or I have not spoken on my own authority; the Father who sent me has himself given me commandment what to say and what to speak. And I know that his commandment is eternal

A SERIES OF JESUS' POWERFUL WORDS

life. What I say, therefore, I say as the Father has bidden me.

(John 12, 49. 50)

Whoever Believes in Jesus Should Not Perish but Have Eternal Life

Jesus (to Nicodemus):

nd as Moses lifted up the serpent in the wilderness, so must the Son of man be lifted up, that whoever believes in him may have eternal life. For God so loved the world that he gave his only Son, that whoever believes in him should not perish but have eternal life.

(John 3, 14 - 16)

He Who Believes in the Son Has Eternal Life

John the Baptist:

e who believes in the Son has eternal life; he who does not obey the Son shall not see life, but the wrath of God rests upon him.

(John 3, 36)

If Any One Keeps My Word, He Will Never See Death

Jesus (to the Jews):

ruly, truly, I say to you, if any one keeps my word, he will never see death.

(John 8, 51)

THE TEACHINGS OF JESUS

Come to Me That You May Have Life

Jesus (to the Jews):

ou refuse to come to me that you may have life.

(John 5, 40)

Whoever Lives and Believes in Me Shall Never Die

Jesus (to Martha):

am the resurrection and the life; he who believes in me, though he die, yet shall he live, and whoever lives and believes in me shall never die.

(John 11, 25. 26)

He Who Believes Has Eternal Life

Jesus (to the Jews):

ruly, truly, I say to you, he who believes has eternal life.

(John 6, 47)

He Who Have Followed Me Will Receive a Hundredfold, and Inherit Eternal Life

Peter (to Jesus):

o, we have left everything and followed you. What then shall we have?

Jesus said to them:

A SERIES OF JESUS' POWERFUL WORDS

♦ *Truly, I say to you, in the new world, when the Son of man shall sit on his glorious throne, you who have followed me will also sit on twelve thrones, judging the twelve tribes of Israel. And every one who has left houses or brothers or sisters or father or mother or children or lands, for my name's sake, will receive a hundred fold, and inherit eternal life. But many that are first will be last, and the last first.*

(Matthew 19, 27 - 30; Mark 10, 28 - 31; Luke 18, 28 - 30; 22, 30)

He Who Eats This Bread Will Live for Ever

Jesus (to the Jews):

e who eats my flesh and drinks my blood abides in me, and I in him. As the living Father sent me, and I live because of the Father, so he who eats me will live because of me. This is the bread which came down from heaven, not such as the fathers ate and died; he who eats this bread will live for ever.

(John 6, 56 - 58)

You May Believe That Jesus Is the Christ, the Son of God, and That Believing You May Have Life in His Name

John the Apostle:

ow Jesus did many other signs in the presence of the disciples, which are not written in this book; but these are written that you may believe that Jesus is the Christ, the Son of God, and that believing you may have life in his name.

(John 20, 30. 31)

I Know Them, and They Follow Me
and I Give Them Eternal Life

Jesus (to the Jews):

y sheep hear my voice, and I know them, and they follow me; and I give them eternal life, and they shall never perish, and no one shall snatch them out of my hand.

(John 10, 27. 28)

ENVY

Out of the Heart of Man
Come Evil Thoughts

nd he (Jesus) called the people to him again, and said to them:

♦ *Hear me, all of you, and understand: there is nothing outside a man which by going into him can defile him; but the things which come out of a man are what defile him.*

And when he had entered the house, and left the people, his disciples asked him about the parable. And he said to them:

♦ *Then are you also without understanding? Do you not see that whatever goes into a man from outside cannot defile him, since it enters, not his heart but his stomach, and so passes on?*

(Thus he declared all foods clean.)

And he said:

♦ *What comes out of a man is what defiles a man. For from within, out of the heart of man, come evil thoughts, fornication, theft, murder, adultery, coveting, wickedness, deceit, licentiousness, envy,*

A SERIES OF JESUS' POWERFUL WORDS

slander, pride, foolishness. All these evil things come from within, and they defile a man.

(Mark 7, 14 - 23;   Matthew 15, 10 - 20)

EUCHARIST

This Is My Blood of the Covenant, Which Is Poured Out for Many for the Forgiveness of Sins

ow as they were eating, Jesus took bread, and blessed, and broke it, and gave it to the disciples and said:

♦ *Take, eat; this is my body.*

And he took a cup, and when he had given thanks he gave it to them, saying:

♦ *Drink of it, all of you; for this is my blood of the covenant, which is poured out for many for the forgiveness of sins. I tell you I shall not drink again of this fruit of the vine until that day when I drink it new with you in my Father's kingdom.*

And when they had sung a hymn, they went out to the Mount of Olives.

(Matthew 26, 26 - 30;   Mark 14, 22 - 27;   Luke 22, 14 - 20)

EVIL

Do Not Resist One Who Is Evil

(The Sermon on the Mount)

Jesus (to his disciples and the crowds):

ou have heard that it was said, `An eye for an eye and a tooth for a tooth.' But I say to you, Do not resist one who is evil. But if any one strikes you on the right cheek, turn *to him the other also; and if any one would sue you and take your coat, let him have your cloak as well; and if any one forces you to go one mile, go with him two miles.*

(Matthew 5, 38 - 41; Luke 6, 29)

EVIL THINGS

The Things Which Come Out of a Man Are What Defile Him

And he (Jesus) called the people to him again, and said to them:

♦ *Hear me, all of you, and understand: there is nothing outside a man which by going into him can defile him; but the things which come out of a man are what defile him.*

And when he had entered the house, and left the people, his disciples asked him about the parable. And he said to them:

♦ *Then are you also without understanding? Do you not see that whatever goes into a man from outside cannot defile him, since it enters, not his heart but his stomach, and so passes on?*

(Thus he declared all foods clean.)

And he said:

♦ *What comes out of a man is what defiles a man. For from within, out of the heart of man, come evil thoughts, fornication, theft, murder, adultery, coveting, wickedness, deceit, licentiousness, envy, slander, pride, foolishness. All these evil things come from within, and they defile a man.*

(Mark 7, 14 - 23;   Matthew 15, 10 - 20)

All Who Take the Sword Will Perish by the Sword

Jesus (to one of his disciples):

ut your sword back into its place; for all who take the sword will perish by the sword.

(Matthew 26, 52; Mark 14, 47; Luke 22, 50)

EXALTED

What Is Exalted Among Men Is an Abomination in the Sight of God

Jesus (to the Pharisees):

ou are those who justify yourselves before men, but God knows your hearts; for what is exalted among men is an abomination in the sight of God.

(Luke 16, 15)

Every One Who Exalts Himself Will Be Humbled

ne sabbath when he went to dine at the house of a ruler who belonged to the Pharisees, they were watching him. Now he told a parable to those who were invited, when he marked how they chose the places of honor, saying to them:

♦ *When you are invited by any one to a marriage feast, do not sit down in a place of honor, lest a more eminent man than you be invited by him; and he who invited you both will come and say to you, `Give place to this man,' and then you will begin with shame to take the lowest place. But when you are invited, go and sit in*

THE TEACHINGS OF JESUS

the lowest place, so that when your host comes he may say to you, `Friend, go up higher'; then you will be honored in the presence of all who sit at table with you. For every one who exalts himself will be humbled, and he who humbles himself will be exalted.

(Luke 14, 1. 7 - 11; Matthew 23, 12; Luke 18, 14)

Whoever Exalts Himself Will Be Humbled

Jesus (to his disciples):

e who is greatest among you shall be your servant; whoever exalts himself will be humbled, and whoever humbles himself will be exalted.

(Matthew 23, 11 - 12)

EYE

Your Eye Is the Lamp of Your Body

Jesus (to his disciples and the crowds):

our eye is the lamp of your body; when your eye is sound, your whole body is full of light; but when it is not sound, your body is full of darkness. Therefore be careful lest the light in you be darkness. If then your whole body is full of light, having no part dark, it will be wholly bright, as when a lamp with its rays gives you light.

(Luke 11, 34 - 36)

♦ *If your eye is not sound, your whole body will be full of darkness. If then the light in you is darkness, how great is the darkness!*

(Matthew 6, 23)

A SERIES OF JESUS' POWERFUL WORDS

FAITH

A Faith As a Grain of Mustard Seed

he apostles said to the Lord:

♦ *Increase our faith!*

And the Lord said:

♦ *If you had faith as a grain of mustard seed, you could say to this sycamine tree, `Be rooted up, and be planted in the sea,' and it would obey you.*

(Luke 17, 5. 6)

A Little Faith As a Grain of Mustard Seed

hen the disciples came to Jesus privately and said:

♦ *Why could we not cast it out?*

He said to them:

♦ *Because of your little faith. For truly, I say to you, if you have faith as a grain of mustard seed, you will say to this mountain, `Move from here to there,' and it will move; and nothing will be impossible to you.*

(Matthew 17, 19. 20)

And when he (Jesus) had entered the house, his disciples asked him privately:

♦ *Why could we not cast it out?*

And he said to them:

THE TEACHINGS OF JESUS

♦ *This kind cannot be driven out by anything but prayer.*

(Mark 9, 28. 29)

Blessed Are Those Who Have Not Seen and yet Believe

Jesus (to Thomas):

ave you believed because you have seen me? Blessed are those who have not seen and yet believe.

(John 20, 29)

If My Words Abide in You, Ask Whatever You Will

Jesus (to his disciples):

f you abide in me, and my words abide in you, ask whatever you will, and it shall be done for you. By this my Father is glorified, that you bear much fruit, and so prove to be my disciples.

(John 15, 7. 8)

FAITHFUL

He Who Is Faithful in a Very Little Is Faithful Also in Much

Jesus (to his disciples):

e who is faithful in a very little is faithful also in much; and he who is dishonest in a very little is dishonest also in much.

(Luke 16, 10; 19, 17; Matthew 25, 21)

A SERIES OF JESUS' POWERFUL WORDS

Woe to You, When All Men Speak Well of You
(The Sermon on the Mount)

Jesus (to his disciples and a great multitude
of people from all Judea and Jerusalem
and the seacost of Tyre and Sidon):

oe to you, when all men speak well of you, for so their fathers did to the false prophets.

(Luke 6, 26)

FALSE PROPHETS

Woe to You, When All Men Speak Well of You
(The Sermon on the Mount)

Jesus (to his disciples and a great multitude
of people from all Judea and Jerusalem
and the seacost of Tyre and Sidon):

oe to you, when all men speak well of you, for so their fathers did to the false prophets.

(Luke 6, 26)

Beware of False Prophets
(The Sermon on the Mount)

Jesus (to his disciples and the crowds):

eware of false prophets, who come to you in sheep's clothing but inwardly are ravenous wolves. You will know them by their fruits. Are grapes gathered from thorns, or figs from thistles? So, every sound tree bears good fruit, but the bad

THE TEACHINGS OF JESUS

tree bears evil fruit. A sound tree cannot bear evil fruit, nor can a bad tree bear good fruit. Every tree that does not bear good fruit is cut down and thrown into the fire. Thus you will know them by their fruits.

(Matthew 7, 15 - 20)

Take Heed That No One
Leads You Astray

s he (Jesus) sat on the Mount of Olives, the disciples came to him privately, saying:

♦ *Tell us, when will this be, and what will be the sign of your coming and of the close of the age?*

And Jesus answered them:

♦ *Take heed that no one leads you astray. For many will come in my name, saying, `I am the Christ,' and they will lead many astray.*

(Matthew 24, 3 - 5. 11;   Mark 13, 3 - 6;   Luke 21, 7. 8)

FALSE WITNESS

You Shall Not Bear False Witness

Jesus (to the rich young man):

*f you would enter life, keep the commandments.*

He said to him:

♦ *Which?*

And Jesus said:

You shall not kill, You shall not commit adultery, You shall not steal, You shall not bear false witness, Honor your father and mother, and, You shall love your neighbor as yourself.

The young man said to him:

♦ *All these I have observed; what do I still lack?*

Jesus said to him:

♦ *If you would be perfect, go, sell what you possess and give to the poor, and you will have treasure in heaven; and come, follow me.*

When the young man heard this he went away sorrowful; for he had great possessions.

(Matthew 19, 17 - 22;   Mark 10, 19 - 22;   Luke 18, 20 - 23)

FAST

The Wedding Guests Do Not Fast While the Bridegroom Is with Them

ow John's disciples and the Pharisees were fasting; and people came and said to him (Jesus):

♦ *Why do John's disciples and the disciples of the Pharisees fast, but your disciples do not fast?*

And Jesus said to them:

♦ *Can the wedding guests fast while the bridegroom is with them? As long as they have the bridegroom with them, they cannot fast. The days will come, when the bridegroom is taken away from them and then they will fast in that day.*

No one sews a piece of unshrunk cloth on an old garment; if he does, the patch tears away from it, the new from the old, and a worse tear

THE TEACHINGS OF JESUS

is made. And no one puts new wine into old wineskins; if he does, the wine will burst the skins, and the wine is lost, and so are the skins; but new wine is for fresh skins.

(Mark 2, 18 - 22; Matthew 9, 14 - 17; Luke 5, 33 - 39)

When You Fast, Do Not Look Dismal, Like the Hypocrites
(The Sermon on the Mount)

Jesus (to his disciples and the crowds):

nd when you fast, do not look dismal, like the hypocrites, for they disfigure their faces that their fasting may be seen by men. Truly, I say to you, they have received their reward. But when you fast, anoint your head and wash your face, that your fasting may not be seen by men but by your Father who is in secret; and your Father who sees in secret will reward you.

(Matthew 6, 16 - 18)

FATHER AND MOTHER

Honor Your Father and Mother

nd behold, one came up to him (Jesus) , saying:

♦ *Teacher, what good deed must I do, to have eternal life?*

And he said to him:

♦ *Why do you ask me about what is good? One there is who is good. If you would enter life, keep the commandments.*

He said to him:

♦ *Which?*

A SERIES OF JESUS' POWERFUL WORDS

And Jesus said:

♦ *You shall not kill, You shall not commit adultery, You shall not steal, You shall not bear false witness, Honor your father and mother, and, You shall love your neighbor as yourself.*

The young man said to him:

♦ *All these I have observed; what do I still lack?*

Jesus said to him:

♦ *If you would be perfect, go, sell what you possess and give to the poor, and you will have treasure in heaven; and come, follow me.*

When the young man heard this he went away sorrowful; for he had great possessions.

(Matthew 19, 16 - 22; Mark 10, 19 - 22; Luke 18, 20 - 23)

Whoever of You Does Not Renounce All That He Has Cannot Be My Disciple

How great multitudes accompanied him (Jesus); and he turned and said to them:

♦ *If any one comes to me and does not hate his own father and mother and wife and children and brothers and sisters, yes, and even his own life, he cannot be my disciple. Whoever does not bear his own cross and come after me, cannot be my disciple. So therefore, whoever of you does not renounce all that he has cannot be my disciple.*

(Luke 14, 25 - 27, 33; Matthew 10, 37;   16, 24; Mark 8, 34. 35; Luke 9, 23)

THE TEACHINGS OF JESUS

He Who Loves Father or Mother More Than Me Is Not Worthy of Me

Jesus (to his disciples):

e who loves father or mother more than me is not worthy of me; and he who loves son or daughter more than me is not worthy of me.

(Matthew 10, 37; Luke 14, 26)

Honor Your Father and Your Mother

Jesus (to the Pharisees):

nd he (Jesus) said to them:

- *You have a fine way of rejecting the commandment of God, in order to keep your tradition! For Moses said, `Honor your father and your mother'; and, `He who speaks evil of father or mother, let him surely die'*

(Mark 7, 9. 10)

Every One Who Has Left All, for My Name's Sake, Will Receive a Hundredfold, and Inherit Eternal Life

Peter (to Jesus):

o, we have left everything and followed you. What then shall we have?

Jesus said to them:

- *Truly, I say to you, in the new world, when the Son of man shall*

A SERIES OF JESUS' POWERFUL WORDS

sit on his glorious throne, you who have followed me will also sit on twelve thrones, judging the twelve tribes of Israel. And every one who has left houses or brothers or sisters or father or mother or children or lands, for my name's sake, will receive a hundred fold, and inherit eternal life. But many that are first will be last, and the last first.

(Matthew 19, 27 - 30; Mark 10, 28 - 31; Luke 18, 28 - 30; 22, 30)

FATHER'S WILL

Not One of the Sparrows Will Fall to the Ground Without Your Father's Will

Jesus (to his disciples):

re not two sparrows sold for a penny? And not one of them will fall to the ground without your Father's will. But even the hairs of your head are all numbered. Fear not, therefore; you are of more value than many sparrows.

(Matthew 10, 29 - 31; Luke 12, 6. 7)

FEAR

You Are of More Value Than Many Sparrows

Jesus (to his disciples):

re not two sparrows sold for a penny? And not one of them will fall to the ground without your Father's will. But even the hairs of your head are all numbered. Fear not, therefore; you are of more value than many sparrows.

(Matthew 10, 29 - 31; Luke 12, 6. 7)

THE TEACHINGS OF JESUS

Fear Him Who, After He Has Killed, Has Power to Cast into Hell

Jesus (to his disciples):

 *tell you, my friends, do not fear those who kill the body, and after that have no more that they can do. But I will warn you whom to fear: fear him who, after he has killed, has power to cast into hell; yes, I tell you, fear him!*

(Luke 12, 4. 5; Matthew 10, 28)

FIG

From the Fig Tree Learn Its Lesson

Jesus (to his disciples):

or as the lightning comes from the east and shines as far as the west, so will be the coming of the Son of man. Wherever the body is, there the eagles will be gathered together.

Immediately after the tribulation of those days the sun will be darkened, and the moon will not give its light, and the stars will fall from heaven, and the powers of the heavens will be shaken; then will appear the sign of the Son of man in heaven, and then all the tribes of the earth will mourn, and they will see the Son of man coming on the clouds of heaven with power and great glory; and he will send out his angels with a loud trumpet call, and they will gather his elect from the four winds, from one end of heaven to the other.

From the fig tree learn its lesson: as soon as its branch becomes tender and puts forth its leaves, you know that summer is near. So also, when you see all these things, you know that he is near, at the very gates.

(Matthew 24, 27 - 33; Mark 13, 24 - 29; Luke 21, 25 - 31)

FIRST

If Any One Would Be First

Jesus (to his disciples):

f any one would be first, he must be last of all and servant of all.

(Mark 9, 35)

He Who Is Greatest Among You

Jesus (to his disciples):

e who is greatest among you shall be your servant; whoever exalts himself will be humbled, and whoever humbles himself will be exalted.

(Matthew 23, 11 - 12)

Some Are First Who Will Be Last

e (Jesus) went on his way through towns and villages, teaching, and journeying toward Jerusalem. And some one said to him:

♦ *Lord, will those who are saved be few?*

And he said to them:

♦ *Strive to enter by the narrow door; for many, I tell you, will seek to enter and will not be able.*

When once the householder has risen up and shut the door, you will begin to stand outside and to knock at the door, saying, `Lord, open to us.' He will answer you, `I do not know where you

THE TEACHINGS OF JESUS

come from.' Then you will begin to say, `We ate and drank in your presence, and you taught in our streets.' But he will say, `I tell you, I do not know where you come from; depart from me, all you workers of iniquity!' There you will weep and gnash your teeth, when you see Abraham and Isaac and Jacob and all the prophets in the kingdom of God and you yourselves thrust out.

And men will come from east and west, and from north and south, and sit at table in the kingdom of God. And behold, some are last who will be first, and some are first who will be last.

(Luke 13, 22 - 30)

FLESH

The Spirit Indeed Is Willing, but the Flesh Is Weak

Jesus (to Peter, James and John):

atch and pray that you may not enter into temptation; the spirit indeed is willing, but the flesh is weak.

(Matthew 26, 41; Mark 14, 38; Luke 22, 46)

He Who Eats My Flesh and Drinks My Blood I Will Raise Him Up at the Last Day

Jesus (to the Jews):

ruly, truly, I say to you, unless you eat the flesh of the Son of man and drink his blood, you have no life in you; he who eats my flesh and drinks my blood has eternal life, and I will raise him up at the last day. For my flesh is foo indeed, and my blood is drink indeed.

(John 6, 53 - 55)

A SERIES OF JESUS' POWERFUL WORDS

FOOD

Is Not Life More Than Food, and the Body More Than Clothing?

(The Sermon on the Mount)

Jesus (to his disciples and the crowds):

herefore I tell you, do not be anxious about your life, what you shall eat or what you shall drink, nor about your body, what you shall put on. Is not life more than food, and the body more than clothing? Look at the birds of the air: they neither sow nor reap nor gather into barns, and yet your heavenly Father feeds them. Are you not of more value than they?

And which of you by being anxious can add one cubit to his span of life?

And why are you anxious about clothing? Consider the lilies of the field, how they grow; they neither toil nor spin; yet I tell you, even Solomon in all his glory was not arrayed like one of these. But if God so clothes the grass of the field, which today is alive and tomorrow is thrown into the oven, will he not much more clothe you, O men of little faith?

Therefore do not be anxious, saying, `What shall we eat?' or ` What shall we drink?' or `What shall we wear?' For the Gentiles seek all these things; and your heavenly Father knows that you need them all. But seek first his kingdom and his righteousness, and all these things shall be yours as well.

Therefore do not be anxious about tomorrow, for tomorrow will be anxious for itself. Let the day's own trouble be sufficient for the day.

(Matthew 6, 25 - 34; Luke 12, 22 - 31)

THE TEACHINGS OF JESUS

FOOLISHNESS

Out of the Heart of Man, Come Evil Thoughts

And he (Jesus) called the people to him again, and said to them:

♦ *Hear me, all of you, and understand: there is nothing outside a man which by going into him can defile him; but the things which come out of a man are what defile him.*

And when he had entered the house, and left the people, his disciples asked him about the parable. And he said to them:

♦ *Then are you also without understanding? Do you not see that whatever goes into a man from outside cannot defile him, since it enters, not his heart but his stomach, and so passes on?*

(Thus he declared all foods clean.)

And he said:

♦ *What comes out of a man is what defiles a man. For from within, out of the heart of man, come evil thoughts, fornication, theft, murder, adultery, coveting, wickedness, deceit, licentiousness, envy, slander, pride, foolishness. All these evil things come from within, and they defile a man.*

(Mark 7, 14 - 23;   Matthew 15, 10 - 20)

A SERIES OF JESUS' POWERFUL WORDS

FORGIVE

If You Do Not Forgive Men Their Trespasses, Neither Will Your Father Forgive Your Trespasses

(The Sermon on the Mount)

Jesus (to his disciples and the crowds):

or if you forgive men their trespasses, your heavenly Father also will forgive you; but if you do not forgive men their trespasses, neither will your Father forgive your trespasses.

(Matthew 6, 14. 15; Mark 11, 25. 26; Luke 6, 37)

Forgive, if You Have Anything Against Any One

Jesus (to his disciples):

nd whenever you stand praying, forgive, if you have anything against any one; so that your Father also who is in heaven may forgive you your trespasses.

(Mark 11, 25)

If Your Brother Sins, Rebuke Him, and if He Repents, Forgive Him

Jesus (to his disciples):

ake heed to yourselves; if your brother sins, rebuke him, and if he repents, forgive him; and if he sins against you seven times in the day, and turns to you seven times, and says, `I repent,' you must forgive him.

(Luke 17, 3. 4)

THE TEACHINGS OF JESUS

How Often Shall My Brother Sin Against Me

hen Peter came up and said to him (Jesus):

♦ *Lord, how often shall my brother sin against me, and I forgive him? As many as seven times?*

Jesus said to him:

♦ *I do not say to you seven times, but seventy times seven.*

(Matthew 18, 21. 22)

FORNICATION

Out of the Heart of Man, Come Evil Thoughts

nd he (Jesus) called the people to him again, and said to them:

♦ *Hear me, all of you, and understand: there is nothing outside a man which by going into him can defile him; but the things which come out of a man are what defile him.*

And when he had entered the house, and left the people, his disciples asked him about the parable. And he said to them:

♦ *Then are you also without understanding? Do you not see that whatever goes into a man from outside cannot defile him, since it enters, not his heart but his stomach, and so passes on?*

(Thus he declared all foods clean.)

And he said:

♦ *What comes out of a man is what defiles a man. For from within,*

A SERIES OF JESUS' POWERFUL WORDS

out of the heart of man, come evil thoughts, fornication, theft, murder, adultery, coveting, wickedness, deceit, licentiousness, envy, slander, pride, foolishness. All these evil things come from within, and they defile a man.

(Mark 7, 14 - 23;   Matthew 15, 10 - 20)

FULL

Woe to You That Are Full Now

(The Sermon on the Mount)

nd he (Jesus) came down with them and stood on a level place, with a great crowd of his disciples and a great multitude of people from all Judea and Jerusalem and the seacoast of Tyre and Sidon, who came to hear him and to be healed of their diseases; and those who were troubled with unclean spirits were cured. And all the crowd sought to touch him, for power came forth from him and healed them all. And he lifted up his eyes on his disciples, and said:

♦ *Woe to you that are full now, for you shall hunger.*

(Luke 6, 17 - 20. 25)

GATE (DOOR)

Strive to Enter by the Narrow Door

e (Jesus) went on his way through towns and villages, teaching, and journeying toward Jerusalem. And some one said to him:

♦ *Lord, will those who are saved be few?*

And he said to them:

♦ *Strive to enter by the narrow door; for many, I tell you, will seek to enter and will not be able.*

When once the householder has risen up and shut the door, you will begin to stand outside and to knock at the door, saying, `Lord, open to us.'

He will answer you, `I do not know where you come from.'

Then you will begin to say, `We ate and drank in your presence, and you taught in our streets.'

But he will say, `I tell you, I do not know where you come from; depart from me, all you workers of iniquity!' There you will weep and gnash your teeth, when you see Abraham and Isaac and Jacob and all the prophets in the kingdom of God and you yourselves thrust out.

And men will come from east and west, and from north and south, and sit at table in the kingdom of God. And behold, some are last who will be first, and some are first who will be last.

(Luke 13, 22 - 30)

Enter by the Narrow Gate

(The Sermon on the Mount)

Jesus (to his disciples and the crowds):

 *nter by the narrow gate; for the gate is wide and the way is easy, that leads to destruction, and those who enter by it are many. For the gate is narrow and the way is hard, that leads to life, and those who find it are few.*

(Matthew 7, 13. 14; Luke 13, 24)

A SERIES OF JESUS' POWERFUL WORDS

GENTILES

If Your Brother Refuses to Listen Let Him Be To You As a Gentile and a Tax Collector

Jesus (to his disciples):

f your brother sins against you, go and tell him his fault, between you and him alone. If he listens to you, you have gained your brother. But if he does not listen, take one or two others along with you, that every word may be confirmed by the evidence of two or three witnesses. If he refuses to listen to them, tell it to the church; and if he refuses to listen even to the church, let him be to you as a Gentile and a tax collector.

(Matthew 18, 15 - 17)

The Gentiles Are Anxious, Saying `What Shall We Eat?' or `What Shall We Drink?' or `What Shall We Wear?

(The Sermon on the Mount)

Jesus (to his disciples and the crowds):

herefore I tell you, do not be anxious about your life, what you shall eat or what you shall drink, nor about your body, what you shall put on. Is not life more than food, and the body more than clothing?

Look at the birds of the air: they neither sow nor reap nor gather into barns, and yet your heavenly Father feeds them. Are you not of more value than they?

And which of you by being anxious can add one cubit to his span of life?

And why are you anxious about clothing?

Consider the lilies of the field, how they grow; they neither toil nor spin; yet I tell you, even Solomon in all his glory was not arrayed like one of these. But if God so clothes the grass of the field, which today is alive and tomorrow is thrown into the oven, will he not much more clothe you, O men of little faith?

Therefore do not be anxious, saying, `What shall we eat?' or ` What shall we drink?' or `What shall we wear?'

For the Gentiles seek all these things; and your heavenly Father knows that you need them all. But seek first his kingdom and his righteousness, and all these things shall be yours as well.

Therefore do not be anxious about tomorrow, for tomorrow will be anxious for itself. Let the day's own trouble be sufficient for the day.

(Matthew 6, 25 - 34; Luke 12, 22 - 31)

GENTLE

I Am Gentle and Lowly in Heart

Jesus (to his disciples and the crowds):

ome to me, all who labor and are heavy laden, and I will give you rest.

Take my yoke upon you, and learn from me; for I am gentle and lowly in heart, and you will find rest for your souls.

For my yoke is easy, and my burden is light.

(Matthew 11, 28 - 30)

A SERIES OF JESUS' POWERFUL WORDS

GIVE

Give, and It Will Be Given to You
(The Sermon on the Mount)

Jesus (to his disciples and a great multitude
of people from all Judea and Jerusalem
and the seacost of Tyre and Sidon):

ive, and it will be given to you; good measure, pressed down, shaken together, running over, will be put into your lap. For the measure you give will be the measure you get back.

(Luke 6, 38; Mark 4, 24)

To Him Who Has Will More Be Given

Jesus (to his disciples):

ake heed then how you hear; for to him who has will more be given, and from him who has not, even what he thinks that he has will be taken away.

(Luke 8, 18; Mark 4, 25)

For to Him Who Has Will More Be Given

Jesus (to his disciples):

ake heed what you hear; the measure you give will be the measure you get, and still more will be given you. For to him who has will more be given; and from him who has not, even what he has will be taken away.

(Mark 4, 24. 25; Luke 8, 18)

THE TEACHINGS OF JESUS

Give to Every One Who Begs from You
(The Sermon on the Mount)

Jesus (to his disciples and a great multitude
　　　of people from all Judea and Jerusalem
　　　and the seacost of Tyre and Sidon):

ive to every one who begs from you; and of him who takes away your goods do not ask them again.

(Luke 6, 30;　Matthew 5, 42)

It Is More Blessed to Give

Jesus (to his disciples):

t is more blessed to give than to receive.

(Acts 20, 35)

GLORY

They Will See the Son of Man Coming on the Clouds of Heaven with Power and Great Glory

Jesus (to his disciples):

or as the lightning comes from the east and shines as far as the west, so will be the coming of the Son of man. Wherever the body is, there the eagles will be gathered together.

Immediately after the tribulation of those days the sun will be darkened, and the moon will not give its light, and the stars will fall from heaven, and the powers of the heavens will be shaken; then will appear the sign of the Son of man in heaven, and then all the tribes of the earth will mourn, and they will see the Son of man coming on the clouds of heaven with power and great glory; and he will send out his angels with a loud trumpet call, and they will gather his elect from the four winds, from one end of heaven to the other.

(Matthew 24, 27 - 31; Mark 13, 24 - 27)

GOD

You Cannot Serve God and Mammon

(The Sermon on the Mount)

Jesus (to his disciples and the crowds):

o one can serve two masters; for either he will hate the one and love the other, or he will be devoted to the one and despise the other.

You cannot serve God and mammon.

(Matthew 6, 24; Luke 16, 13)

GOD'S WILL

Not One of Them Will Fall to the Ground Without Your Father's Will

Jesus (to his disciples):

re not two sparrows sold for a penny? And not one of them will fall to the ground without your Father's will.

But even the hairs of your head are all numbered. Fear not, therefore; you are of more value than many sparrows.

(Matthew 10, 29 - 31; Luke 12, 6. 7)

THE TEACHINGS OF JESUS

GREATEST

The Greatest in the Kingdom of Heaven?

t that time the disciples came to Jesus, saying:

♦ *Who is the greatest in the kingdom of heaven?*

And calling to him a child, he put him in the midst of them, and said:

♦ *Truly, I say to you, unless you turn and become like children, you will never enter the kingdom of heaven. Whoever humbles himself like this child, he is the greatest in the kingdom of heaven. Whoever receives one such child in my name receives me; but whoever causes one of these little ones who believe in me to sin, it would be better for him to have a great millstone fastened round his neck and to be drowned in the depth of the sea.*

Woe to the world for temptations to sin! For it is necessary that temptations come, but woe to the man by whom the temptation comes!

(Matthew 18, 1 - 7; Mark 9, 35 - 37; Luke 9, 46 - 48)

Who Is Greatest Among You Shall Be Your Servant

Jesus (to his disciples):

e who is greatest among you shall be your servant; whoever exalts himself will be humbled, and whoever humbles himself will be exalted.

(Matthew 23, 11. 12; Luke 14, 11; 18, 14)

GUILT

If You Were Blind, You Would Have No Guilt

Jesus (to a man blind from his birth):

or judgment I came into this world, that those who do not see may see, and that those who see may become blind.

Some of the Pharisees near him heard this, and they said to him:

♦ *Are we also blind?*

Jesus said to them:

♦ *If you were blind, you would have no guilt; but now that you say, 'We see,' your guilt remains.*

(John 9, 39 - 41)

HARVEST

I Sent You to Reap

Jesus (to his disciples):

o you not say, 'There are yet four months, then comes the harvest'? I tell you, lift up your eyes, and see how the fields are already white for harvest. He who reaps receives wages, and gathers fruit for eternal life, so that sower and reaper may rejoice together. For here the saying holds true, 'One sows and another reaps.'

I sent you to reap that for which you did not labor; others have labored, and you have entered into their labor.

(John 4, 35 - 38)

Pray to the Lord of the Harvest to Send Out Laborers into His Harvest

hen he saw the crowds, he had compassion for them, because they were harassed and helpless, like sheep without a shepherd. Then he said to his disciples:

♦ *The harvest is plentiful, but the laborers are few; pray therefore the Lord of the harvest to send out laborers into his harvest.*

(Matthew 9, 36 - 38; Luke 10, 2)

HATE

You Have Heard `Hate Your Enemy` but I Say to You `Love Your Enemies`
(The Sermon on the Mount)

Jesus (to his disciples and the crowds):

ou have heard that it was said, `You shall love your neighbor and hate your enemy.' But I say to you, Love your enemies and pray for those who persecute you, so that you may be sons of your Father who is in heaven; for he makes his sun rise on the evil and on the good, and sends rain on the just and on the unjust.

For if you love those who love you, what reward have you? Do not even the tax collectors do the same?

And if you salute only your brethren, what more are you doing than others? Do not even the Gentiles do the same? You, therefore, must be perfect, as your heavenly Father is perfect.

(Matthew 5, 43 - 48; Luke 6, 27. 28. 32. 35. 36)

A SERIES OF JESUS' POWERFUL WORDS

They Have Seen and Hated both Me and My Father

Jesus (to his disciples):

f I had not done among them the works which no one else did, they would not have sin; but now they have seen and hated both me and my Father.

(John 15, 24)

You Will Be Hated by All for My Name's Sake

Jesus (to his disciples):

rother will deliver up brother to death, and the father his child, and children will rise against parents and have them put to death; and you will be hated by all for my name's sake. But he who endures to the end will be saved.

(Matthew 10, 21. 22;   24, 9;   Mark 13, 12. 13;   Luke 21, 16. 17)

Every One Who Does Evil Hates the Light

Jesus (to Nicodemus):

nd this is the judgment, that the light has come into the world, and men loved darkness rather than light, because their deeds were evil. For every one who does evil hates the light, and does not come to the light, lest his deeds should be exposed. But he who does what is true comes to the light, that it may be clearly seen that his deeds have been wrought in God.

(John 3, 19 - 21)

The World Hates Me Because I Testify
of It That Its Works Are Evil

Jesus (to his brothers):

he world cannot hate you, but it hates me because I testify of it that its works are evil. Go to the feast yourselves; I am not going up to this feast, for my time has not yet fully come.

(John 7, 7. 8)

Because You Are Not of the World,
Therefore the World Hates You

Jesus (to his disciples):

f the world hates you, know that it has hated me before it hated you. If you were of the world, the world would love its own; but because you are not of the world, but I chose you out of the world, therefore the world hates you.

Remember the word that I said to you, `A servant is not greater than his master.' If they persecuted me, they will persecute you; if they kept my word, they will keep yours also. But all this they will do to you on my account, because they do not know him who sent me.

(John 15, 18 - 21)

A SERIES OF JESUS' POWERFUL WORDS

HEAD OF THE CORNER

The Very Stone Which the Builders Rejected Has Become the Head of the Corner

Jesus (to the chief Priests and the Pharisees):

ave you never read in the scriptures: 'The very stone which the builders rejected has become the head of the corner; this was the Lord's doing, and it is marvelous in our eyes'?

Therefore I tell you, the kingdom of God will be taken away from you and given to a nation producing the fruits of it.

(Matthew 21, 42. 43; Mark 12, 10. 11; Luke 20; 17. 18)

HEARS

The Hairs of Your Head Are All Numbered

Jesus (to his disciples):

re not two sparrows sold for a penny? And not one of them will fall to the ground without your Father's will. But even the hairs of your head are all numbered. Fear not, therefore; you are of more value than many sparrows.

(Matthew 10, 29 - 31; Luke 12, 6. 7)

HEART OF MAN

Blessed Are the Pure in Heart

(The Sermon on the Mount)

nd great crowds followed him (Jesus) from Galilee and the Decapolis and Jerusalem and Judea and from beyond the Jordan. Seeing the crowds, he went up on the mountain, and

THE TEACHINGS OF JESUS

when he sat down his disciples came to him. And he opened his mouth and taught them, saying:

♦ *Blessed are the pure in heart, for they shall see God.*

(Matthew 4, 25; 5, 1. 2. 8)

I Am Gentle And Lowly in Heart

Jesus (to his disciples and the crowds):

ome to me, all who labor and are heavy laden, and I will give you rest. Take my yoke upon you, and learn from me; for I am gentle and lowly in heart, and you will find rest for your souls. For my yoke is easy, and my burden is light.

(Matthew 11, 28 - 30)

Where Your Treasure Is, There Will Your Heart Be Also
(The Sermon on the Mount)

nd great crowds followed him (Jesus) from Galilee and the Decapolis and Jerusalem and Judea and from beyond the Jordan. Seeing the crowds, he went up on the mountain, and when he sat down his disciples came to him. And he opened his mouth and taught them, saying:

♦ *Do not lay up for yourselves treasures on earth, where moth and rust consume and where thieves break in and steal, but lay up for yourselves treasures in heaven, where neither moth nor rust consumes and where thieves do not break in and steal.*

For where your treasure is, there will your heart be also.

(Matthew 4, 25; 5, 1. 2; 6, 19 - 21; Luke 6, 17 - 20; 12, 33. 34)

A SERIES OF JESUS' POWERFUL WORDS

Out of the Abundance of the Heart His Mouth Speaks
(The Sermon on the Mount)

Jesus (to his disciples and a great multitude
of people from all Judea and Jerusalem
and the seacost of Tyre and Sidon):

he good man out of the good treasure of his heart produces good, and the evil man out of his evil treasure produces evil; for out of the abundance of the heart his mouth speaks.

(Luke 6, 45;   Matthew 12, 34. 35)

Out of the Heart of Man, Come Evil Things

nd he (Jesus) called the people to him again, and said to them:

♦ *Hear me, all of you, and understand: there is nothing outside a man which by going into him can defile him; but the things which come out of a man are what defile him.*

And when he had entered the house, and left the people, his disciples asked him about the parable. And he said to them:

♦ *Then are you also without understanding? Do you not see that whatever goes into a man from outside cannot defile him, since it enters, not his heart but his stomach, and so passes on?*

(Thus he declared all foods clean.)

And he said:

♦ *What comes out of a man is what defiles a man. For from within, out of the heart of man, come evil thoughts, fornication, theft, murder, adultery, coveting, wickedness, deceit, licentiousness, envy, slander, pride, foolishness. All these evil things come from within, and they defile a man.*

(Mark 7, 14 - 23;   Matthew 15, 10 - 20)

Take Heed to Yourselves Lest Your Hearts Be Weighed Down with Dissipation and Drunkenness and Cares of This Life

Jesus (to his disciples):

ut take heed to yourselves lest your hearts be weighed down with dissipation and drunkenness and cares of this life, and that day come upon you suddenly like a snare; for it will come upon all who dwell upon the face of the whole earth.

But watch at all times, praying that you may have strength to escape all these things that will take place, and to stand before the Son of man.

(Luke 21, 34 - 36;   Matthew 24, 42;   25, 13;   Mark 13, 33)

This People Honors Me with Their Lips, but Their Heart Is Far from Me

Jesus (to the Pharisees and the scribes):

ell did Isaiah prophesy of you hypocrites, as it is written, `This people honors me with their lips, but their heart is far from me; in vain do they worship me, teaching as doctrines the precepts of men.' You leave the commandment of God, and hold fast the tradition of men.

(Mark 7, 6 - 8;   Matthew 15, 8)

A SERIES OF JESUS' POWERFUL WORDS

God Knows Your Hearts

Jesus (to the Pharisees):

ou are those who justify yourselves before men, but God knows your hearts; for what is exalted among men is an abomination in the sight of God.

(Luke 16, 15)

You Shall Love the Lord Your God with All Your Heart

Jesus (to one of the scribes):

he first (commandment) is, `Hear, O Israel: The Lord our God, the Lord is one; and you shall love the Lord your God with all your heart, and with all your soul, and with all your mind, and with all your strength.' The second is this, `You shall love your neighbor as yourself.' There is no other commandment greater than these.

(Mark 12, 29 - 31; Matthew 22, 37)

HIDDEN

Nothing Is Hidden That Will Not Be Known

n the meantime, when so many thousands of the multitude had gathered together that they trod upon one another, he (Jesus) began to say to his disciples first:

♦ *Beware of the leaven of the Pharisees, which is hypocrisy. Nothing is covered up that will not be revealed, or hidden that will not be known. Therefore whatever you have said in the dark*

THE TEACHINGS OF JESUS

shall be heard in the light, and what you have whispered in private rooms shall be proclaimed upon the housetops.

(Luke 12, 1 - 3)

HOLY

Do Not Throw Your Pearls Before Swine

(The Sermon on the Mount)

nd great crowds followed him (Jesus) from Galilee and the Decapolis and Jerusalem and Judea and from beyond the Jordan. Seeing the crowds, he went up on the mountain, and when he sat down his disciples came to him. And he opened his mouth and taught them, saying:

♦ *Do not give dogs what is holy; and do not throw your pearls before swine, lest they trample them under foot and turn to attack you.*

(Matthew 4, 25; 5, 1. 2; 7, 6)

HOLY COVENANT

This Is My Blood of the Covenant, Which Is Poured Out for Many for the Forgiveness of Sins

ow as they were eating, Jesus took bread, and blessed, and broke it, and gave it to the disciples and said:

♦ *Take, eat; this is my body.*

And he took a cup, and when he had given thanks he gave it to them, saying:

♦ *Drink of it, all of you; for this is my blood of the covenant, which is poured out for many for the forgiveness of sins. I tell you I shall*

A SERIES OF JESUS' POWERFUL WORDS

not drink again of this fruit of the vine until that day when I drink it new with you in my Father's kingdom.

And when they had sung a hymn, they went out to the Mount of Olives.

(Matthew 26, 26 - 30; Mark 14, 22 - 27; Luke 22, 14 - 20)

HOLY SPIRIT

Whoever Blasphemes Against the Holy Spirit Never Has Forgiveness

Jesus (to his disciples and the crowds):

ruly, I say to you, all sins will be forgiven the sons of men, and whatever blasphemies they utter; but whoever blasphemes against the Holy Spirit never has forgiveness, but is guilty of an eternal sin.

(Mark 3, 28. 29)

Whoever Speaks Against the Holy Spirit Will Not Be Forgiven

Jesus (to his disciples and the crowds):

herefore I tell you, every sin and blasphemy will be forgiven men, but the blasphemy against the Spirit will not be forgiven.

And whoever says a word against the Son of man will be forgiven; but whoever speaks against the Holy Spirit will not be forgiven, either in this age or in the age to come.

(Matthew 12, 31. 32)

HONOR

Honor Your Father and Mother

nd behold, one came up to him (Jesus), saying:

♦ *Teacher, what good deed must I do, to have eternal life?*

And he said to him:

♦ *Why do you ask me about what is good? One there is who is good. If you would enter life, keep the commandments.*

He said to him:

♦ *Which?*

And Jesus said:

♦ *You shall not kill, You shall not commit adultery, You shall not steal, You shall not bear false witness, Honor your father and mother, and, You shall love your neighbor as yourself.*

The young man said to him:

♦ *All these I have observed; what do I still lack?*

Jesus said to him:

♦ *If you would be perfect, go, sell what you possess and give to the poor, and you will have treasure in heaven; and come, follow me.*

When the young man heard this he went away sorrowful; for he had great possessions. And Jesus said to his disciples:

♦ *Truly, I say to you, it will be hard for a rich man to enter the kingdom of heaven.*

(Matthew 19, 16 - 23;   Mark 10, 19 - 23;   Luke 18, 18 - 24)

A SERIES OF JESUS' POWERFUL WORDS

Honor Your Father and Your Mother

Jesus (to the Pharisees):

nd he (Jesus) said to them:

- *You have a fine way of rejecting the commandment of God, in order to keep your tradition! For Moses said, `Honor your father and your mother'; and, `He who speaks evil of father or mother, let him surely die'*

(Mark 7, 9. 10)

HUMBLE

Whoever Humbles Himself Will Be Exalted

Jesus (to his disciples):

e who is greatest among you shall be your servant; whoever exalts himself will be humbled, and whoever humbles himself will be exalted.

(Matthew 23, 11. 12;   Luke 14, 11;   18, 14)

He Who Humbles Himself Will Be Exalted

ne sabbath when he went to dine at the house of a ruler who belonged to the Pharisees, they were watching him. Now he told a parable to those who were invited, when he marked how they chose the places of honor, saying to them:

- *When you are invited by any one to a marriage feast, do not sit down in a place of honor, lest a more eminent man than you be*

THE TEACHINGS OF JESUS

invited by him; and he who invited you both will come and say to you, `Give place to this man,' and then you will begin with shame to take the lowest place. But when you are invited, go and sit in the lowest place, so that when your host comes he may say to you, `Friend, go up higher'; then you will be honored in the presence of all who sit at table with you. For every one who exalts himself will be humbled, and he who humbles himself will be exalted.

(Luke 14, 1. 7 - 11; Matthew 23, 12; Luke 18, 14)

We Are Unworthy Servants

Jesus (to his disciples):

ill any one of you, who has a servant plowing or keeping sheep, say to him when he has come in from the field, `Come at once and sit down at table'?

Will he not rather say to him, `Prepare supper for me, and gird yourself and serve me, till I eat and drink; and afterward you shall eat and drink'? Does he thank the servant because he did what was commanded?

So you also, when you have done all that is commanded you, say, `We are unworthy servants; we have only done what was our duty.

(Luke 17, 7 - 10)

I Am Among You As One Who Serves

Jesus (to his disciples):

or which is the greater, one who sits at table, or one who serves? Is it not the one who sits at table? But I am among you as one who serves. You are those who have continued with me in my trials; and I assign to you, as my Father assigned to me, a kingdom, that you may eat and drink at my table in my kingdom, and sit on thrones judging the twelve tribes of Israel.

(Luke 22, 27 - 30)

To Be Humble Like a Child

t that time the disciples came to Jesus, saying:

♦ *Who is the greatest in the kingdom of heaven?*

And calling to him a child, he put him in the midst of them, and said:

♦ *Truly, I say to you, unless you turn and become like children, you will never enter the kingdom of heaven.*

Whoever humbles himself like this child, he is the greatest in the kingdom of heaven.

Whoever receives one such child in my name receives me; but whoever causes one of these little ones who believe in me to sin, it would be better for him to have a great millstone fastened round his neck and to be drowned in the depth of the sea.

(Matthew 18, 1 - 6; Mark 9, 35 - 37; Luke 9, 46 - 48)

If Any One Would Be First, He Must Be Last of All

Jesus (to his disciples):

*f any one would be first, he must be last of all and servant of all.*

(Mark 9, 35)

THE TEACHINGS OF JESUS

Whoever Would Be First Among You Must Be Your Slave

nd when the ten heard it (the mother of the sons of Zebedee asked Jesus: "Command that these two sons of mine may sit, one at your right hand and one at your left, in your kingdom") they were indignant at the two brothers.

But Jesus called them to him and said:

♦ *You know that the rulers of the Gentiles lord it over them, and their great men exercise authority over them. It shall not be so among you; but whoever would be great among you must be your servant, and whoever would be first among you must be your slave; even as the Son of man came not to be served but to serve, and to give his life as a ransom for many.*

(Matthew 20, 24 - 28; Mark 9, 35; 10, 41 - 45; Luke 22, 24 - 26)

HUNGER

Blessed Are Those Who Hunger and Thirst for Righteousness

(The Sermon on the Mount)

nd great crowds followed him (Jesus) from Galilee and the Decapolis and Jerusalem and Judea and from beyond the Jordan. Seeing the crowds, he went up on the mountain, and when he sat down his disciples came to him. And he opened his mouth and taught them, saying:

♦ *Blessed are those who hunger and thirst for righteousness, for they shall be satisfied.*

(Matthew 4, 25; 5, 1. 2. 6; Luke 6, 17 - 21)

A SERIES OF JESUS' POWERFUL WORDS

HYPOCRITE

Beware of the Leaven of the Pharisees, Which Is Hypocrisy

n the meantime, when so many thousands of the multitude had gathered together that they trod upon one another, he (Jesus) began to say to his disciples first:

♦ *Beware of the leaven of the Pharisees, which is hypocrisy. Nothing is covered up that will not be revealed, or hidden that will not be known. Therefore whatever you have said in the dark shall be heard in the light, and what you have whispered in private rooms shall be proclaimed upon the housetops.*

(Luke 12, 1 - 3)

Does Not Each of You on the Sabbath Untie His Ox or His Ass from the Manger

ut the ruler of the synagogue, indignant because Jesus had healed on the sabbath, said to the people:

♦ *There are six days on which work ought to be done; come on those days and be healed, and not on the sabbath day.*

Then the Lord answered him:

♦ *You hypocrites! Does not each of you on the sabbath untie his ox or his ass from the manger, and lead it away to water it? And ought not this woman, a daughter of Abraham whom Satan bound for eighteen years, be loosed from this bond on the sabbath day?*

As he said this, all his adversaries were put to shame; and all the people rejoiced at all the glorious things that were done by him.

(Luke 13, 14 - 17)

You Hypocrite, First Take the Log Out of Your Own Eye

(The Sermon on the Mount)

nd great crowds followed him (Jesus) from Galilee and the Decapolis and Jerusalem and Judea and from beyond the Jordan. Seeing the crowds, he went up on the mountain, and when he sat down his disciples came to him. And he opened his mouth and taught them, saying:

♦ *Why do you see the speck that is in your brother's eye, but do not notice the log that is in your own eye? Or how can you say to your brother, `Let me take the speck out of your eye,' when there is the log in your own eye?*

You hypocrite, first take the log out of your own eye, and then you will see clearly to take the speck out of your brother's eye.

(Matthew 4, 25; 5, 1. 2; 7, 3 - 5; Luke 6, 17 - 21; 41. 42)

JERUSALEM

Jerusalem Will Be Trodden Down by the Gentiles

Jesus (to his disciples):

ut when you see Jerusalem surrounded by armies, then know that its desolation has come near.

Then let those who are in Judea flee to the mountains, and let those who are inside the city depart, and let not those who are out in the country enter it; for these are days of vengeance, to fulfil all that is written.

Alas for those who are with child and for those who give suck in those days! For great distress shall be upon the earth and wrath upon this people; they will fall by the edge of the sword, and be led captive among all nations; and Jerusalem will be trodden down by the Gentiles, until the times of the Gentiles are fulfilled.

(Luke 21, 20 - 24;   Mark 13, 14 - 20;   Matthew 24, 15 - 22)

There Shall Not Be Left Here One Stone Upon Another

And as some spoke of the temple, how it was adorned with noble stones and offerings, he (Jesus) said:

♦ *As for these things which you see, the days will come when there shall not be left here one stone upon another that will not be thrown down.*

(Luke 21, 5. 6;   Matthew 24, 1. 2 ;   Mark 13, 1. 2)

You Did Not Know the Time of Your Visitation

And when he (Jesus) drew near and saw the city (Jerusalem) he wept over it, saying:

♦ *Would that even today you knew the things that make for peace! But now they are hid from your eyes.*

For the days shall come upon you, when your enemies will cast up a bank about you and surround you, and hem you in on every side, and dash you to the ground, you and your children within you, and they will not leave one stone upon another in you; because you did not know the time of your visitation.

(Luke 19, 41 - 44;   Matthew 24, 2;   Mark 13, 2)

O Jerusalem, Jerusalem, Killing the Prophets

Jesus (to the Pharisees):

Jerusalem, Jerusalem, killing the prophets and stoning those who are sent to you! How often would I have gathered your children together as a hen gathers her brood under her wings, and you would not! Behold, your house is forsaken. And I tell you, you will not see me until you say, `Blessed is he who comes in the name of the Lord!

(Luke 13, 34. 35; Matthew 23, 37 - 39)

JESUS CHRIST, THE SON OF GOD

These Signs Are Written That You May Believe That Jesus Is the Christ, the Son Of God

John the Apostle:

ow Jesus did many other signs in the presence of the disciples, which are not written in this book; but these are written that you may believe that Jesus is the Christ, the Son of God, and that believing you may have life in his name.

(John 20, 30. 31)

JUDGEMENT

I Did Not Come to Judge the World but to Save the World

Jesus (to his disciples and the crowds):

e who believes in me, believes not in me but in him who sent me. And he who sees me sees him who sent me. I have come as light into the world, that whoever believes in me may not

A SERIES OF JESUS' POWERFUL WORDS

remain in darkness. *If any one hears my sayings and does not keep them, I do not judge him; for I did not come to judge the world but to save the world.*

(John 12, 44 - 47)

Judge Not, That You Be Not Judged
(The Sermon on the Mount)

Jesus (to his disciples and the crowds):

udge not, that you be not judged. For with the judgment you pronounce you will be judged, and the measure you give will be the measure you get.

(Matthew 7, 1. 2; Luke 6, 37)

He Who Hears My Word and Believes Him Who Sent Me, Does Not Come into Judgment

Jesus (to the Jews):

ruly, truly, I say to you, he who hears my word and believes him who sent me, has eternal life; he does not come into judgment, but has passed from death to life.

(John 5, 24)

For Judgment I Came into This World

Jesus (to a man blind from his birth):

or judgment I came into this world, that those who do not see may see, and that those who see may become blind.

Some of the Pharisees near him heard this, and they said

to him:

♦ *Are we also blind?*

Jesus said to them:

♦ *If you were blind, you would have no guilt; but now that you say, 'We see,' your guilt remains.*

(John 9, 39 - 41)

Now Is the Judgment of This World, Now Shall the Ruler of This World Be Cast Out

Jesus (to his disciples and the crowds):

ow is the judgment of this world, now shall the ruler of this world be cast out; and I, when I am lifted up from the earth, will draw all men to myself.

(John 12, 31. 32)

Woe to You Chorazin and Bethsaida on the Day of Judgment

hen he (Jesus) began to upbraid the cities where most of his mighty works had been done, because they did not repent:

♦ *Woe to you, Chorazin! woe to you, Bethsaida! for if the the mighty works done in you had been done in Tyre and Sidon, they would have repented long ago in sackcloth and ashes. But I tell you, it shall be more tolerable on the day of judgment for Tyre and Sidon than for you. And you, Capernaum, will you be exalted to heaven? You shall be brought down to Hades. For if the mighty works done in you had been done in Sodom, it would have remained until this day. But I tell you that it shall be more tolerable on the day of judgment for the land of Sodom than for you.*

(Matthew 11, 20 - 24; Luke 10, 13. 14)

Whoever Kills Shall Be Liable to Judgment
(The Sermon on the Mount)

Jesus (to his disciples and the crowds):

ou have heard that it was said to the men of old, 'You shall not kill; and whoever kills shall be liable to judgment.' But I say to you that every one who is angry with his brother shall be liable to judgment; whoever insults his brother shall be liable to the council, and whoever says, 'You fool!' shall be liable to the hell of fire.

So if you are offering your gift at the altar, and there remember that your brother has something against you, leave your gift there before the altar and go; first be reconciled to your brother, and then come and offer your gift.

(Matthew 5, 21 - 24)

JUSTIFIED

By Your Words You Will Be Justified

Jesus (to the Pharisees):

tell you, on the day of judgment men will render account for every careless word they utter; for by your words you will be justified, and by your words you will be condemned.

(Matthew 12, 36. 37)

KILL

You Shall Not Kill

Jesus (to the rich young man):

 *If you would enter life, keep the commandments.*

He said to him:

- *Which?*

And Jesus said:

- *You shall not kill, You shall not commit adultery, You shall not steal, You shall not bear false witness, Honor your father and mother, and, You shall love your neighbor as yourself.*

The young man said to him:

- *All these I have observed; what do I still lack?*

Jesus said to him:

- *If you would be perfect, go, sell what you possess and give to the poor, and you will have treasure in heaven; and come, follow me.*

When the young man heard this he went away sorrowful; for he had great possessions.

And Jesus said to his disciples:

- *Truly, I say to you, it will be hard for a rich man to enter the kingdom of heaven. Again I tell you, it is easier for a camel to go through the eye of a needle than for a rich man to enter the kingdom of God.*

When the disciples heard this they were greatly astonished, saying:

- *Who then can be saved?*

A SERIES OF JESUS' POWERFUL WORDS

But Jesus looked at them and said to them:

♦ *With men this is impossible, but with God all things are possible.*

(Matthew 19, 17 - 26; Mark 10, 19 - 27; Luke 18, 20 - 27)

KINGDOM OF GOD

I Assign to You a Kingdom

Jesus (to his disciples):

or which is the greater, one who sits at table, or one who serves? Is it not the one who sits at table? But I am among you as one who serves. You are those who have continued with me in my trials; and I assign to you, as my Father assigned to me, a kingdom, that you may eat and drink at my table in my kingdom, and sit on thrones judging the twelve tribes of Israel.

(Luke 22, 27 - 30)

Seek First the Kingdom of God and His Righteousness
(The Sermon on the Mount)

Jesus (to his disciples and the crowds):

herefore I tell you, do not be anxious about your life, what you shall eat or what you shall drink, nor about your body, what you shall put on. Is not life more than food, and the body more than clothing?

Look at the birds of the air: they neither sow nor reap nor gather into barns, and yet your heavenly Father feeds them. Are you not of more value than they?

And which of you by being anxious can add one cubit to his span of life?

And why are you anxious about clothing? Consider the lilies of the field, how they grow; they neither toil nor spin; yet I tell you, even Solomon in all his glory was not arrayed like one of these. But if God so clothes the grass of the field, which today is alive and tomorrow is thrown into the oven, will he not much more clothe you, O men of little faith?

Therefore do not be anxious, saying, `What shall we eat?' or ` What shall we drink?' or `What shall we wear?' For the Gentiles seek all these things; and your heavenly Father knows that you need them all. But seek first his kingdom and his righteousness, and all these things shall be yours as well.

Therefore do not be anxious about tomorrow, for tomorrow will be anxious for itself. Let the day's own trouble be sufficient for the day.

(Matthew 6, 25 - 34; Luke 12, 22 - 31)

No One Who Puts His Hand to the Plow and Looks Back Is Fit for the Kingdom of God

s they (Jesus and his disciples) were going along the road, a man said to him:

♦ *I will follow you wherever you go.*

And Jesus said to him:

♦ *Foxes have holes, and birds of the air have nests; but the Son of man has nowhere to lay his head.*

To another he said:

A SERIES OF JESUS' POWERFUL WORDS

♦ *Follow me.*

But he said:

♦ *Lord, let me first go and bury my father.*

But he said to him:

♦ *Leave the dead to bury their own dead; but as for you, go and proclaim the kingdom of God.*

Another said:

♦ *I will follow you, Lord; but let me first say farewell to those at my home.*

Jesus said to him:

♦ *No one who puts his hand to the plow and looks back is fit for the kingdom of God.*

(Luke 9, 57 - 62)

It Is Easier for a Camel to Go Through the Eye of a Needle Than for a Rich Man to Enter the Kingdom of God

Jesus (to his disciples):

ruly, I say to you, it will be hard for a rich man to enter the kingdom of heaven. Again I tell you, it is easier for a camel to go through the eye of a needle than for a rich man to enter the kingdom of God.

When the disciples heard this they were greatly astonished, saying:

♦ *Who then can be saved?*

But Jesus looked at them and said to them:

The Kingdom of God Will Be Taken Away from You and Given to a Nation Producing the Fruits of It

Jesus (to the chief Priests and the Pharisees):

ave you never read in the scriptures: 'The very stone which the builders rejected has become the head of the corner; this was the Lord's doing, and it is marvelous in our eyes'?

Therefore I tell you, the kingdom of God will be taken away from you and given to a nation producing the fruits of it.

(Matthew 21, 42 - 44; Mark 12, 10. 11; Luke 20; 17. 18)

The Kingdom of God Is Not Coming with Signs to Be Observed

eing asked by the Pharisees when the kingdom of God was coming, he (Jesus) answered them:

♦ *The kingdom of God is not coming with signs to be observed; nor will they say, `Lo, here it is!' or `There!' for behold, the kingdom of God is in the midst of you."*

(Luke 17, 20. 21)

The Kingdom of God Has Come Upon You

hen a blind and dumb demoniac was brought to him (Jesus), and he healed him, so that the dumb man spoke and saw. And all the people were amazed, and said:

A SERIES OF JESUS' POWERFUL WORDS

♦ *Can this be the Son of David?*

But when the Pharisees heard it they said:

♦ *It is only by Beelzebul, the prince of demons, that this man casts out demons.*

Knowing their thoughts, he said to them:

♦ *Every kingdom divided against itself is laid waste, and no city or house divided against itself will stand; and if Satan casts out Satan, he is divided against himself; how then will his kingdom stand? And if I cast out demons by Beelzebul, by whom do your sons cast them out? Therefore they shall be your judges.*

But if it is by the Spirit of God that I cast out demons, then the kingdom of God has come upon you.

Or how can one enter a strong man's house and plunder his goods, unless he first binds the strong man? Then indeed he may plunder his house.

(Matthew 12, 22 - 29; Mark 3, 22 – 27; Luke 11, 14 – 22)

The Kingdom of Heaven Has Suffered Violence

As they (two disciples of John the Baptist) went away, Jesus began to speak to the crowds concerning John:

♦ *What did you go out into the wilderness to behold? A reed shaken by the wind? From the days of John the Baptist until now the kingdom of heaven has suffered violence, and men of violence take it by force. For all the prophets and the law prophesied until John.*

(Matthew 11, 7. 12. 13 ; Luke 16, 16)

Not Every One Who Says to Me, `Lord, Lord,' Shall Enter the Kingdom of Heaven

(The Sermon on the Mount)

Jesus (to his disciples and the crowds):

ot every one who says to me, `Lord, Lord,' shall enter the kingdom of heaven, but he who does the will of my Father who is in heaven.

On that day many will say to me, `Lord, Lord, did we not prophesy in your name, and cast out demons in your name, and do many mighty works in your name?' And then will I declare to them, `I never knew you; depart from me, you evildoers.'

(Matthew 7, 21 - 23; Luke 6, 46)

Seek First Kingdom and His Righteousness

(The Sermon on the Mount)

Jesus (to his disciples and the crowds):

herefore I tell you, do not be anxious about your life, what you shall eat or what you shall drink, nor about your body, what you shall put on. Is not life more than food, and the body more than clothing?

Look at the birds of the air: they neither sow nor reap nor gather into barns, and yet your heavenly Father feeds them. Are you not of more value than they?

And which of you by being anxious can add one cubit to his span of life?

And why are you anxious about clothing? Consider the lilies of the field, how they grow; they neither toil nor spin; yet I tell you, even Solomon in all his glory was not arrayed like one of these. But if God so clothes the grass of the field, which today is alive and tomorrow is thrown into the oven, will he not much more clothe you, O men of little faith?

Therefore do not be anxious, saying, `What shall we eat?' or `What shall we drink?' or `What shall we wear?' For the Gentiles seek all these things; and your heavenly Father knows that you need them all. But seek first his kingdom and his righteousness, and all these things shall be yours as well.

Therefore do not be anxious about tomorrow, for tomorrow will be anxious for itself. Let the day's own trouble be sufficient for the day.

(Matthew 6, 25 - 34; Luke 12, 22 - 31)

Who Is the Greatest in the Kingdom of Heaven?

At that time the disciples came to Jesus, saying:

♦ *Who is the greatest in the kingdom of heaven?*

And calling to him a child, he put him in the midst of them, and said:

♦ *Truly, I say to you, unless you turn and become like children, you will never enter the kingdom of heaven.*

Whoever humbles himself like this child, he is the greatest in the kingdom of heaven.

Whoever receives one such child in my name receives me; but who-

THE TEACHINGS OF JESUS

ever causes one of these little ones who believe in me to sin, it would be better for him to have a great millstone fastened round his neck and to be drowned in the depth of the sea.

(Matthew 18, 1 - 6; Mark 9, 35 - 37; Luke 9, 46 - 48)

It Will Be Hard for a Rich Man to Enter the Kingdom of Heaven

Jesus (to his disciples):

ruly, I say to you, it will be hard for a rich man to enter the kingdom of heaven. Again I tell you, it is easier for a camel to go through the eye of a needle than for a rich man to enter the kingdom of God.

(Matthew 19, 23. 24; Mark 10, 23. 25; Luke 18, 24, 25)

It Is Your Father's Good Pleasure to Give You the Kingdom

Jesus (to his disciples and the Jews):

ear not, little flock, for it is your Father's good pleasure to give you the kingdom.

(Luke 12, 32)

Whoever Does Not Receive the Kingdom of God Like a Child Shall Not Enter It

nd they (his disciples) were bringing children to him (Jesus), that he might touch them; and the disciples rebuked them. But when Jesus saw it he was indignant, and said to them:

♦ *Let the children come to me, do not hinder them; for to such belongs the kingdom of God. Truly, I say to you, whoever does not receive the kingdom of God like a child shall not enter it.*

And he took them in his arms and blessed them, laying his hands upon them.

(Mark 10, 13 - 16; Matthew 19, 13. 14; 18, 3; Luke 18, 15 - 17)

Many Will Come from East and West

centurion (to Jesus):

♦ *Lord, my servant is lying paralyzed at home, in terrible distress.*

And he said to him:

♦ *I will come and heal him.*

But the centurion answered him:

♦ *Lord, I am not worthy to have you come under my roof; but only say the word, and my servant will be healed. For I am a man under authority, with soldiers under me; and I say to one, `Go,' and he goes, and to another, `Come,' and he comes, and to my slave, `Do this,' and he does it.*

When Jesus heard him, he marveled, and said to those who followed him:

♦ *Truly, I say to you, not even in Israel have I found such faith. I tell you, many will come from east and west and sit at table with Abraham, Isaac, and Jacob in the kingdom of heaven, while the sons of the kingdom will be thrown into the outer darkness; there men will weep and gnash their teeth.*

(Matthew 8, 6 - 12; Luke 7, 2 - 9)

How to Enter the Kingdom of Heaven?
(The Sermon on the Mount)

Jesus (to his disciples and the crowds):

or I tell you, unless your righteousness exceeds that of the scribes and Pharisees, you will never enter the kingdom of heaven.

(Matthew 5, 20)

KNOCK

Every One Who Asks Receives, and He Who Seeks Finds, and to Him Who Knocks It Will Be Opened
(The Sermon on the Mount)

Jesus (to his disciples and the crowds):

sk, and it will be given you; seek, and you will find; knock, and it will be opened to you. For every one who asks receives, and he who seeks finds, and to him who knocks it will be opened.

Or what man of you, if his son asks him for bread, will give him a stone? Or if he asks for a fish, will give him a serpent? If you then, who are evil, know how to give good gifts to your children, how much more will your Father who is in heaven give good things to those who ask him!

(Matthew 7, 7 - 11; Luke 11, 9 - 13)

A SERIES OF JESUS' POWERFUL WORDS

LABOR

All Who Labor and Are Heavy Laden, I Will Give You Rest

Jesus (to his disciples and the crowds):

ome to me, all who labor and are heavy laden, and I will give you rest. Take my yoke upon you, and learn from me; for I am gentle and lowly in heart, and you will find rest for your souls. For my yoke is easy, and my burden is light.

(Matthew 11, 28 - 30)

LADEN

All Who Labor and Are Heavy Laden, I Will Give You Rest

Jesus (to his disciples and the crowds):

ome to me, all who labor and are heavy laden, and I will give you rest. Take my yoke upon you, and learn from me; for I am gentle and lowly in heart, and you will find rest for your souls. For my yoke is easy, and my burden is light.

(Matthew 11, 28 - 30)

LAME

When You Give a Feast, Invite the Poor, the Maimed, the Lame, the Blind

ne sabbath when he (Jesus) went to dine at the house of a ruler who belonged to the Pharisees, they were watching him. He said also to the man who had invited him:

♦ *When you give a dinner or a banquet, do not invite your friends or your brothers or your kinsmen or rich neighbors, lest they also invite you in return, and you be repaid. But when you give a feast, invite the poor, the maimed, the lame, the blind, and you will be blessed, because they cannot repay you. You will be repaid at the resurrection of the just.*

(Luke 14, 1. 12 - 14)

LAMP

Let Your Light So Shine Before Men, That They May See Your Good Works and Give Glory to Your Father Who Is in Heaven
(The Sermon on the Mount)

Jesus (to his disciples and the crowds):

or do men light a lamp and put it under a bushel, but on a stand, and it gives light to all in the house. Let your light so shine before men, that they may see your good works and give glory to your Father who is in heaven.

(Matthew 5, 15. 16; Mark 4, 21; Luke 8, 16; 11, 33)

Your Eye Is the Lamp of Your Body
(The Sermon on the Mount)

Jesus (to his disciples and the crowds):

our eye is the lamp of your body; when your eye is sound, your whole body is full of light; but when it is not sound, your body is full of darkness. Therefore be careful lest the light in you be darkness. If then your whole body is full of light, having no part dark, it will be wholly bright, as when a lamp

A SERIES OF JESUS' POWERFUL WORDS

with its rays gives you light.

(Luke 11, 34 – 36)

If your eye is not sound, your whole body will be full of darkness. If then the light in you is darkness, how great is the darkness!

(Matthew 6, 23)

LAST

If Any One Would Be First Must Be Last of All

Jesus (to his disciples):

f any one would be first, he must be last of all and servant of all.

(Mark 9, 35)

Some Are Last Who Will Be First

e (Jesus) went on his way through towns and villages, teaching, and journeying toward Jerusalem. And some one said to him:

♦ *Lord, will those who are saved be few?*

And he said to them:

♦ *Strive to enter by the narrow door; for many, I tell you, will seek to enter and will not be able.*

When once the householder has risen up and shut the door, you will begin to stand outside and to knock at the door, saying, `Lord, open to us.' He will answer you, `I do not know where you *come from.' Then you will begin to say, `We ate and drank in your presence, and you taught in our streets.' But he will say, `I tell you, I do not know where you come from; depart from me, all you workers of iniquity!' There you will weep and gnash your teeth, when you see Abraham and Isaac and Jacob and all the prophets in the kingdom of God and you yourselves thrust out.*

And men will come from east and west, and from north and south, and sit at table in the kingdom of God. And behold, some are last who will be first, and some are first who will be last.

(Luke 13, 22 - 30)

LAST DAY

He Who Eats My Flesh and Drinks My Blood I Will Raise Him Up at the Last Day

Jesus (to the Jews):

ruly, truly, I say to you, unless you eat the flesh of the Son of man and drink his blood, you have no life in you; he who eats my flesh and drinks my blood has eternal life, and I will raise him up at the last day. For my flesh is foo indeed, and my blood is drink indeed.

(John 6, 53 - 55)

The Word That I Have Spoken Will Be His Judge on the Last Day

Jesus (to his disciples and the crowds):

f any one hears my sayings and does not keep them, I do not judge him; for I did not come to judge the world but to save the world. He who rejects me and does not receive my sayings has a judge; the word that I have spoken will be his judge on the last day.

(John 12, 47. 48)

That Day Will Come Upon You Suddenly Like a Snare

Jesus (to his disciples):

ut take heed to yourselves lest your hearts be weighed down with dissipation and drunkenness and cares of this life, and that day come upon you suddenly like a snare; for it will come upon all who dwell upon the face of the whole earth.

But watch at all times, praying that you may have strength to escape all these things that will take place, and to stand before the Son of man.

(Luke 21, 34 - 36; Matthew 24, 42; 25, 13; Mark 13, 33)

LAW

Not an Iota, Not a Dot, Will Pass from the Law Until All Is Accomplished
(The Sermon on the Mount)

Jesus (to his disciples and the crowds):

hink not that I have come to abolish the law and the prophets; I have come not to abolish them but to fulfil them. For truly, I say to you, till heaven and earth pass away, not an iota, not a dot, will pass from the law until all is accomplished.

(Matthew 5, 17. 18; Luke 16, 17)

THE TEACHINGS OF JESUS

All the Prophets and the Law Prophesied Until John

s they (two disciples of John the Baptist) went away, Jesus began to speak to the crowds concerning John:

♦ *What did you go out into the wilderness to behold? A reed shaken by the wind? From the days of John the Baptist until now the kingdom of heaven has suffered violence, and men of violence take it by force. For all the prophets and the law prophesied until John.*

(Matthew 11, 7. 12. 13; Luke 16, 16)

Whatever You Wish That Men Would Do to You, Do So to Them
(The Sermon on the Mount)

Jesus (to his disciples and the crowds):

*o whatever you wish that men would do to you, do so to them; for this is the law and the prophets.*

(Matthew 7, 12; Luke 6, 31)

On the First and Second Commandment Depend All the Law and the Prophets
(The Sermon on the Mount)

ut when the Pharisees heard that he (Jesus) had silenced the Sadducees, they came together. And one of them, a lawyer, asked him a question, to test him.

♦ *Teacher, which is the great commandment in the law?*

And he said to him:

A SERIES OF JESUS' POWERFUL WORDS

♦ *You shall love the Lord your God with all your heart, and with all your soul, and with all your mind. This is the great and first commandment.*

And a second is like it, You shall love your neighbor as yourself.

On these two commandments depend all the law and the prophets.

(Matthew 22, 34 - 40; Mark 12; 30. 31; Luke 10, 27)

Do Not Do Good Only to Those Who Do Good to You

(The Sermon on the Mount)

Jesus (to his disciples and a great multitude
of people from all Judea and Jerusalem
and the seacost of Tyre and Sidon):

nd if you do good to those who do good to you, what credit is that to you? For even sinners do the same.

(Luke 6, 33)

LEAVEN

Take Heed and Beware of the Leaven of the Pharisees and Sadducees

Jesus (to his disciples):

ake heed and beware of the leaven of the Pharisees and Sadducees.

And they discussed it among themselves, saying:

♦ *We brought no bread.*

But Jesus, aware of this, said:

♦ *O men of little faith, why do you discuss among yourselves the fact that you have no bread? Do you not yet perceive? Do you not remember the five loaves of the five thousand, and how many baskets you gathered? Or the seven loaves of the four thousand, and how many baskets you gathered? How is it that you fail to perceive that I did not speak about bread? Beware of the leaven of the Pharisees and Sadducees.*

Then they understood that he did not tell them to beware of the leaven of bread, but of the teaching of the Pharisees and Sadducees.

(Matthew 16, 6 - 12; Mark 8, 14 - 21; Luke 12, 1)

Beware of the Leaven of the Pharisees, Which Is Hypocrisy

n the meantime, when so many thousands of the multitude had gathered together that they trod upon one another, he (Jesus) began to say to his disciples first:

♦ *Beware of the leaven of the Pharisees, which is hypocrisy. Nothing is covered up that will not be revealed, or hidden that will not be known. Therefore whatever you have said in the dark shall be heard in the light, and what you have whispered in private rooms shall be proclaimed upon the housetops.*

(Luke 12, 1 - 3)

A SERIES OF JESUS' POWERFUL WORDS

LEND

Sinners Lend to Sinners, to Receive As Much Again

(The Sermon on the Mount)

Jesus (to his disciples and a great multitude
of people from all Judea and Jerusalem
and the seacost of Tyre and Sidon):

nd if you lend to those from whom you hope to receive, what credit is that to you? Even sinners lend to sinners, to receive as much again.

(Luke 6, 34)

LICENTIOUSNESS

Out of the Heart of Man, Come Evil Thoughts

nd he (Jesus) called the people to him again, and said to them:

♦ *Hear me, all of you, and understand: there is nothing outside a man which by going into him can defile him; but the things which come out of a man are what defile him.*

And when he had entered the house, and left the people, his disciples asked him about the parable. And he said to them:

♦ *Then are you also without understanding? Do you not see that whatever goes into a man from outside cannot defile him, since it enters, not his heart but his stomach, and so passes on?*

(Thus he declared all foods clean.)

And he said:

♦ *What comes out of a man is what defiles a man. For from within, out of the heart of man, come evil thoughts, fornication, theft, murder, adultery, coveting, wickedness, deceit, licentiousness, envy, slander, pride, foolishness. All these evil things come from within, and they defile a man.*

(Mark 7, 14 - 23;   Matthew 15, 10 - 20)

LIFE

I Am the Resurrection and the Life

Jesus (to Martha):

am the resurrection and the life; he who believes in me, though he die, yet shall he live, and whoever lives and believes in me shall never die.

(John 11, 25. 26)

Is Not Life More Than Food?

(The Sermon on the Mount)

Jesus (to his disciples and the crowds):

herefore I tell you, do not be anxious about your life, what you shall eat or what you shall drink, nor about your body, what you shall put on. Is not life more than food, and the body more than clothing?

Look at the birds of the air: they neither sow nor reap nor gather into barns, and yet your heavenly Father feeds them. Are you not of more value than they?

And which of you by being anxious can add one cubit to his span

A SERIES OF JESUS' POWERFUL WORDS

of life?

And why are you anxious about clothing? Consider the lilies of the field, how they grow; they neither toil nor spin; yet I tell you, even Solomon in all his glory was not arrayed like one of these. But if God so clothes the grass of the field, which today is alive and tomorrow is thrown into the oven, will he not much more clothe you, O men of little faith?

Therefore do not be anxious, saying, `What shall we eat?' or` What shall we drink?' or `What shall we wear?' For the Gentiles seek all these things; and your heavenly Father knows that you need them all. But seek first his kingdom and his righteousness, and all these things shall be yours as well.

Therefore do not be anxious about tomorrow, for tomorrow will be anxious for itself. Let the day's own trouble be sufficient for the day.

(Matthew 6, 25 - 34; Luke 12, 22 - 31)

It Will Be Hard for a Rich Man to Enter the Kingdom of Heaven

Jesus (to his disciples):

ruly, I say to you, it will be hard for a rich man to enter the kingdom of heaven. Again I tell you, it is easier for a camel to go through the eye of a needle than for a rich man to enter the kingdom of God.

When the disciples heard this they were greatly astonished, saying:

♦ *Who then can be saved?*

But Jesus looked at them and said to them:

THE TEACHINGS OF JESUS

♦ *With men this is impossible, but with God all things are possible.*

(Matthew 19, 23 - 26; Mark 10, 23 - 27; Luke 18, 24 - 27)

He Who Hears My Word and Believes Him Who Sent Me, Has Passed from Death to Life

Jesus (to the Jews):

ruly, truly, I say to you, he who hears my word and believes him who sent me, has eternal life; he does not come into judgment, but has passed from death to life.

(John 5, 24)

How to Gain Your Lives?

Jesus (to his disciples):

y your endurance you will gain your lives.

(Luke 21, 19; Matthew 24, 13)

Whoever Would Save His Life Will Lose It

Jesus (to his disciples):

f any man would come after me, let him deny himself and take up his cross and follow me. For whoever would save his life will lose it, and whoever loses his life for my sake will find it.

(Matthew 16, 24. 25;   10, 38. 39; Mark 8, 34. 35; Luke 9, 23. 24; 17, 33; John 12, 25)

A SERIES OF JESUS' POWERFUL WORDS

He Who Loves His Life Loses It

Jesus (to his disciples):

e who loves his life loses it, and he who hates his life in this world will keep it for eternal life.

(John 12, 25)

What Shall a Man Give in Return for His Life?

Jesus (to his disciples):

or what will it profit a man, if he gains the whole world and forfeits his life? Or what shall a man give in return for his life?

(Matthew 16, 26; Mark 8, 36. 37; Luke 9, 25)

LIGHT

Be Careful Lest the Light in You Be Darkness

(The Sermon on the Mount)

Jesus (to his disciples and the crowds):

our eye is the lamp of your body; when your eye is sound, your whole body is full of light; but when it is not sound, your body is full of darkness. Therefore be careful lest the light in you be darkness. If then your whole body is full of light, having no part dark, it will be wholly bright, as when a lamp with its rays gives you light.

(Luke 11, 34 - 36, Matthew 6, 22. 23)

THE TEACHINGS OF JESUS

I Have Come As Light into the World

Jesus (to his disciples and the crowds):

e who believes in me, believes not in me but in him who sent me. And he who sees me sees him who sent me. I have come as light into the world, that whoever believes in me may not remain in darkness. If any one hears my sayings and does not keep them, I do not judge him; for I did not come to judge the world but to save the world.

(John 12, 44 - 47)

Let Your Light Shine Before Men
(The Sermon on the Mount)

Jesus (to his disciples and the crowds):

or do men light a lamp and put it under a bushel, but on a stand, and it gives light to all in the house. Let your light so shine before men, that they may see your good works and give glory to your Father who is in heaven.

(Matthew 5, 15. 16; Mark 4, 21; Luke 8, 16;   11, 33)

If Any One Walks in the Day, He Does Not Stumble

Jesus (to his disciples):

re there not twelve hours in the day? If any one walks in the day, he does not stumble, because he sees the light of this world. But if any one walks in the night, he stumbles, because the light is not in him.

(John 11, 9. 10)

A SERIES OF JESUS' POWERFUL WORDS

Every One Who Does Evil Hates the Light

Jesus (to Nicodemus):

*nd this is the judgment, that the light has come into the world, and men loved darkness rather than light, because their deeds were evil. For every one who does evil hates the light, and does not come to the light, lest his deeds should be exposed. But he who does what is true comes to the light, that it may be clearly seen that his deeds have been wrought in God.*

(John 3, 19 - 21)

I Am the Light of the World

Jesus (to his disciples and the Jews):

*am the light of the world; he who follows me will not walk in darkness, but will have the light of life.*

(John 8, 12)

You Are the Light of the World

(The Sermon on the Mount)

nd great crowds followed him (Jesus) from Galilee and the Decapolis and Jerusalem and Judea and from beyond the Jordan. Seeing the crowds, he went up on the mountain, and when he sat down his disciples came to him. And he opened his mouth and taught them, saying:

♦ *You are the light of the world. A city set on a hill cannot be hid.*

(Matthew 4, 25; 5, 1. 2. 14)

THE TEACHINGS OF JESUS

Believe in the Light, That You May Become Sons of Light

Jesus (to his disciples and the crowds):

he light is with you for a little longer. Wake while you have the light, lest the darkness overtake you; he who wakes in the darkness does not know where he goes.

While you have the light, believe in the light, that you may become sons of light.

(John 12, 35. 36)

LOG

You Hypocrite, First Take the Log Out of Your Own Eye

(The Sermon on the Mount)

nd great crowds followed him (Jesus) from Galilee and the Decapolis and Jerusalem and Judea and from beyond the Jordan. Seeing the crowds, he went up on the mountain, and when he sat down his disciples came to him. And he opened his mouth and taught them, saying:

♦ *Why do you see the speck that is in your brother's eye, but do not notice the log that is in your own eye?*

Or how can you say to your brother, `Let me take the speck out of your eye,' when there is the log in your own eye?

You hypocrite, first take the log out of your own eye, and then you will see clearly to take the speck out of your brother's eye.

(Matthew 4, 25; 5, 1. 2; 7, 3 - 5; Luke 6, 17 - 21; 41. 42)

A SERIES OF JESUS' POWERFUL WORDS

LORD

You Call Me Teacher and Lord

When he (Jesus) had washed their feet, and taken his garments, and resumed his place, he said to them:

♦ *Do you know what I have done to you? You call me Teacher and Lord; and you are right, for so I am. If I then, your Lord and Teacher, have washed your feet, you also ought to wash one another's feet. For I have given you an example, that you also should do as I have done to you. Truly, truly, I say to you, a servant is not greater than his master; nor is he who is sent greater than he who sent him. If you know these things, blessed are you if you do them.*

I am not speaking of you all; I know whom I have chosen; it is that the scripture may be fulfilled.

(John 13, 12 - 18)

LORD'S SUPPER

This Is My Blood of the Covenant, Which Is Poured Out for Many for the Forgiveness of Sins

Now as they were eating, Jesus took bread, and blessed, and broke it, and gave it to the disciples and said:

♦ *Take, eat; this is my body.*

And he took a cup, and when he had given thanks he gave it to them, saying:

♦ *Drink of it, all of you; for this is my blood of the covenant, which is poured out for many for the forgiveness of sins. I tell you I shall*

THE TEACHINGS OF JESUS

not drink again of this fruit of the vine until that day when I drink it new with you in my Father's kingdom.

And when they had sung a hymn, they went out to the Mount of Olives.

(Matthew 26, 26 - 30; Mark 14, 22 - 27; Luke 22, 14 - 20)

LOVE

Greater Love Has No Man

Jesus (to his disciples):

reater love has no man than this, that a man lay down his life for his friends. You are my friends if you do what I command you.

(John 15, 13. 14)

Love Your Enemies

(The Sermon on the Mount)

Jesus (to his disciples and the crowds):

ou have heard that it was said, `You shall love your neighbor and hate your enemy.' But I say to you, Love your enemies and pray for those who persecute you, so that you may be sons of your Father who is in heaven; for he makes his sun rise on the evil and on the good, and sends rain on the just and on the unjust.

For if you love those who love you, what reward have you? Do not even the tax collectors do the same?

And if you salute only your brethren, what more are you doing than

A SERIES OF JESUS' POWERFUL WORDS

others? Do not even the Gentiles do the same? You, therefore, must be perfect, as your heavenly Father is perfect.

(Matthew 5, 43 - 48; Luke 6, 27. 28. 32. 35. 36)

He Who Loves Me Will Be Loved by My Father

Jesus (to his disciples):

e who has my commandments and keeps them, he it is who loves me; and he who loves me will be loved by my Father, and I will love him and manifest myself to him.

(John 14, 21)

He Who Loves Father or Mother More Than Me Is Not Worthy of Me

Jesus (to his disciples):

e who loves father or mother more than me is not worthy of me; and he who loves son or daughter more than me is not worthy of me.

(Matthew 10, 37; Luke 14, 26)

The First And the Second Commandment
(The Sermon on the Mount)

Jesus (to the rich young man):

ou shall love the Lord your God with all your heart, and with all your soul, and with all your mind. This is the great and first commandment. And a second is like it, You shall love your neighbor as yourself. On these two commandments depend all the law and the prophets.

(Matthew 22, 37 - 40; Mark 12; 30. 31; Luke 10, 27)

A New Commandment I Give to You, That You Love One Another

Jesus (to his disciples):

ittle children, yet a little while I am with you. You will seek me; and as I said to the Jews so now I say to you, `Where I am going you cannot come.'

A new commandment I give to you, that you love one another; even as I have loved you, that you also love one another. By this all men will know that you are my disciples, if you have love for one another.

(John 13, 33 - 35)

LUSTFULLY

Every One Who Looks at a Woman Lustfully Has Already Committed Adultery

(The Sermon on the Mount)

Jesus (to his disciples and the crowds):

ou have heard that it was said, `You shall not commit adultery.' But I say to you that every one who looks at a woman lustfully has already committed adultery with her in his heart.

If your right eye causes you to sin, pluck it out and throw it away; it is better that you lose one of your members than that your whole body be thrown into hell.

(Matthew 5, 27 - 29)

MAIMED

When You Give a Feast, Invite the Poor, the Maimed, the Lame, the Blind

ne sabbath when he (Jesus) went to dine at the house of a ruler who belonged to the Pharisees, they were watching him. He said also to the man who had invited him:

♦ *When you give a dinner or a banquet, do not invite your friends or your brothers or your kinsmen or rich neighbors, lest they also invite you in return, and you be repaid. But when you give a feast, invite the poor, the maimed, the lame, the blind, and you will be blessed, because they cannot repay you. You will be repaid at the resurrection of the just.*

When one of those who sat at table with him heard this, he said to him:

♦ *Blessed is he who shall eat bread in the kingdom of God!*

(Luke 14, 1. 12 - 15)

MAMMON

You Cannot Serve God and Mammon

(The Sermon on the Mount)

Jesus (to his disciples and the crowds):

*o one can serve two masters; for either he will hate the one and love the other, or he will be devoted to the one and despise the other. You cannot serve God and mammon.*

(Matthew 6, 24; Luke 16, 13)

MARRIAGE

The Two Shall Become One Flesh

ow when Jesus had finished these sayings, he went away from Galilee and entered the region of Judea beyond the Jordan; and large crowds followed him, and he healed them there. And Pharisees came up to him and tested him by asking:

♦ *Is it lawful to divorce one's wife for any cause?*

He answered:

♦ *Have you not read that he who made them from the beginning made them male and female, and said, `For this reason a man shall leave his father and mother and be joined to his wife, and the two shall become one flesh'? So they are no longer two but one flesh. What therefore God has joined together, let not man put asunder.*

They said to him:

♦ *Why then did Moses command one to give a certificate of divorce, and to put her away?*

He said to them:

♦ *For your hardness of heart Moses allowed you to divorce your wives, but from the beginning it was not so. And I say to you: whoever divorces his wife, except for unchastity, and marries another, commits adultery.*

The disciples said to him:

♦ *If such is the case of a man with his wife, it is not expedient to marry.*

But he said to them:

♦ *Not all men can receive this saying, but only those to whom it is given. For there are eunuchs who have been so from birth, and there are eunuchs who have been made eunuchs by men, and there are eunuchs who have made themselves eunuchs for the sake of the kingdom of heaven. He who is able to receive this, let him receive it.*

(Matthew 19, 1 - 12; 5, 31. 32; Mark 10, 1 - 12; Luke 16, 18)

MASTER

No One Can Serve Two Masters
(The Sermon on the Mount)

Jesus (to his disciples and the crowds):

o one can serve two masters; for either he will hate the one and love the other, or he will be devoted to the one and despise the other. You cannot serve God and mammon.

(Matthew 6, 24; Luke 16, 13)

A Servant Is Not Greater Than His Master

hen he (Jesus) had washed their feet, and taken his garments, and resumed his place, he said to them:

♦ *Do you know what I have done to you? You call me Teacher and Lord; and you are right, for so I am. If I then, your Lord and Teacher, have washed your feet, you also ought to wash one another's feet. For I have given you an example, that you also should do as I have done to you. Truly, truly, I say to you, a servant is not greater than his master; nor is he who is sent greater than he who sent him. If you know these things, blessed are you if you do them.*

I am not speaking of you all; I know whom I have chosen; it is that the scripture may be fulfilled.

(John 13, 12 - 17)

MEASURE
To Him Who Has, More Will Be Given

Jesus (to his disciples):

ake heed what you hear; the measure you give will be the measure you get, and still more will be given you. For to him who has will more be given; and from him who has not, even what he has will be taken away.

(Mark 4, 24. 25; Luke 8, 18)

The Measure You Give Will Be the Measure You Get
(The Sermon on the Mount)

Jesus (to his disciples and the crowds):

udge not, that you be not judged. For with the judgment you pronounce you will be judged, and the measure you give will be the measure you get.

(Matthew 7, 1. 2; Luke 6, 37)

Judge not, and you will not be judged; condemn not, and you will not be condemned; forgive, and you will be forgiven; give, and it will be given to you; good measure, pressed down, shaken together, running over, will be put into your lap. For the measure you give will be the measure you get back.

(Luke 6, 37. 38; Matthew 7, 1. 2)

A SERIES OF JESUS' POWERFUL WORDS

MEEK

Blessed Are the Meek

(The Sermon on the Mount)

nd great crowds followed him (Jesus) from Galilee and the Decapolis and Jerusalem and Judea and from beyond the Jordan. Seeing the crowds, he went up on the mountain, and when he sat down his disciples came to him. And he opened his mouth and taught them, saying:

♦ *Blessed are the meek, for they shall inherit the earth.*

(Matthew 4, 25; 5, 1. 2. 5)

MERCIFUL

Be Merciful, Even As Your Father Is Merciful

(The Sermon on the Mount)

Jesus (to his disciples and a great multitude
of people from all Judea and Jerusalem
and the seacost of Tyre and Sidon):

nd as you wish that men would do to you, do so to them. If you love those who love you, what credit is that to you? For even sinners love those who love them. And if you do good to those who do good to you, what credit is that to you?

For even sinners do the same. And if you lend to those from whom you hope to receive, what credit is that to you? Even sinners lend to sinners, to receive as much again.

But love your enemies, and do good, and lend, expecting nothing in return; and your reward will be great, and you will be sons of

THE TEACHINGS OF JESUS

the Most High; for he is kind to the ungrateful and the selfish. Be merciful, even as your Father is merciful.

(Luke 6, 31 - 36, Matthew 5, 43 - 48)

I Desire Mercy, and Not Sacrifice

Jesus (to the Pharisees):

nd if you had known what this means, `I desire mercy, and not sacrifice,' you would not have condemned the guiltless.

(Matthew 12, 7)

Go and Learn What This Means, `I Desire Mercy, and Not Sacrifice`

Jesus (to the Pharisees):

hose who are well have no need of a physician, but those who are sick. Go and learn what this means, `I desire mercy, and not sacrifice.' For I came not to call the righteous, but sinners.

(Matthew 9, 12. 13)

Blessed Are the Merciful
(The Sermon on the Mount)

nd great crowds followed him (Jesus) from Galilee and the Decapolis and Jerusalem and Judea and from beyond the Jordan. Seeing the crowds, he went up on the mountain, and when he sat down his disciples came to him. And he opened his mouth and taught them, saying:

A SERIES OF JESUS' POWERFUL WORDS

♦ *Blessed are the merciful, for they shall obtain mercy.*

(Matthew 4, 25; 5, 1. 2. 7)

MOTHER AND FATHER
Honor Your Father and Mother

nd behold, one came up to him (Jesus), saying:

♦ *Teacher, what good deed must I do, to have eternal life?*

And he said to him:

♦ *Why do you ask me about what is good? One there is who is good. If you would enter life, keep the commandments.*

He said to him:

♦ *Which?*

And Jesus said:

♦ *You shall not kill, You shall not commit adultery, You shall not steal, You shall not bear false witness, Honor your father and mother, and, You shall love your neighbor as yourself.*

The young man said to him:

♦ *All these I have observed; what do I still lack?*

Jesus said to him:

♦ *If you would be perfect, go, sell what you possess and give to the poor, and you will have treasure in heaven; and come, follow me.*

When the young man heard this he went away sorrowful; for he had great possessions.

(Matthew 19, 16 - 22; Mark 10, 19 - 22; Luke 18, 20 - 23)

THE TEACHINGS OF JESUS

He Who Loves Father or Mother More Than Me Is Not Worthy of Me

Jesus (to his disciples):

e who loves father or mother more than me is not worthy of me; and he who loves son or daughter more than me is not worthy of me.

(Matthew 10, 37;　Luke 14, 26)

Whoever of You Does Not Renounce All That He Has Cannot Be My Disciple

ow great multitudes accompanied him (Jesus); and he turned and said to them:

♦ *If any one comes to me and does not hate his own father and mother and wife and children and brothers and sisters, yes, and even his own life, he cannot be my disciple. Whoever does not bear his own cross and come after me, cannot be my disciple. So therefore, whoever of you does not renounce all that he has cannot be my disciple.*

(Luke 14, 25 - 27, 33;　Matthew 10, 37;　16, 24;　Mark 8, 34. 35;　Luke 9, 23)

Honor Your Father and Your Mother

Jesus (to the Pharisees):

nd he (Jesus) said to them:

♦ *You have a fine way of rejecting the commandment of God, in order to keep your tradition! For Moses said,*

A SERIES OF JESUS' POWERFUL WORDS

'Honor your father and your mother'; and, 'He who speaks evil of father or mother, let him surely die'

(Mark 7, 9. 10)

Every One Who Has Left All, for My Name's Sake, Will Receive a Hundredfold, and Inherit Eternal Life

Peter (to Jesus):

o, we have left everything and followed you. What then shall we have?

Jesus said to them:

♦ *Truly, I say to you, in the new world, when the Son of man shall sit on his glorious throne, you who have followed me will also sit on twelve thrones, judging the twelve tribes of Israel. And every one who has left houses or brothers or sisters or father or mother or children or lands, for my name's sake, will receive a hundred fold, and inherit eternal life. But many that are first will be last, and the last first.*

(Matthew 19, 27 - 30; Mark 10, 28 - 31; Luke 18, 28 - 30; 22, 30)

MOURN

Blessed Are Those Who Mourn
(The Sermon on the Mount)

nd great crowds followed him (Jesus) from Galilee and the Decapolis and Jerusalem and Judea and from beyond the Jordan. Seeing the crowds, he went up on the mountain, and when he sat down his disciples came to him. And he opened his mouth and taught them, saying:

♦ *Blessed are those who mourn, for they shall be comforted.*

(Matthew 4, 25; 5, 1. 2. 4; Luke 6, 17 - 21)

MURDER

Out of the Heart of Man, Come Evil Thoughts

And he (Jesus) called the people to him again, and said to them:

♦ *Hear me, all of you, and understand: there is nothing outside a man which by going into him can defile him; but the things which come out of a man are what defile him.*

And when he had entered the house, and left the people, his disciples asked him about the parable. And he said to them:

♦ *Then are you also without understanding? Do you not see that whatever goes into a man from outside cannot defile him, since it enters, not his heart but his stomach, and so passes on?*

(Thus he declared all foods clean.)

And he said:

♦ *What comes out of a man is what defiles a man. For from within, out of the heart of man, come evil thoughts, fornication, theft, murder, adultery, coveting, wickedness, deceit, licentiousness, envy, slander, pride, foolishness.*

All these evil things come from within, and they defile a man.

(Mark 7, 14 - 23; Matthew 15, 10 - 20)

MUSTARD SEED

A Faith As a Grain of Mustard Seed

he apostles said to the Lord:

♦ *Increase our faith!*

And the Lord said:

♦ *If you had faith as a grain of mustard seed, you could say to this sycamine tree, `Be rooted up, and be planted in the sea,' and it would obey you.*

(Luke 17, 5. 6)

A Little Faith As a Grain of Mustard Seed

nd when they came to the crowd, a man came up to him (Jesus) and kneeling before him said:

♦ *Lord, have mercy on my son, for he is an epileptic and he suffers terribly; for often he falls into the fire, and often into the water. And I brought him to your disciples, and they could not heal him.*

And Jesus answered:

♦ *O faithless and perverse generation, how long am I to be with you? you? How long am I to bear with you? Bring him here to me.*

And Jesus rebuked him, and the demon came out of him, and the boy was cured instantly.

Then the disciples came to Jesus privately and said:

♦ *Why could we not cast it out?*

He said to them:

♦ *Because of your little faith. For truly, I say to you, if you have faith as a grain of mustard seed, you will say to this mountain, `Move from here to there,' and it will move; and nothing will be impossible to you.*

(Matthew 17, 14 - 21)

NEIGHBOR

You Shall Love Your Neighbor As You Love Yourself

Jesus (to the rich young man):

 *f you would enter life, keep the commandments.*

He said to him:

♦ *Which?*

And Jesus said:

♦ *You shall not kill,*
You shall not commit adultery,
You shall not steal,
You shall not bear false witness,
Honor your father and mother, and,
You shall love your neighbor as yourself.

The young man said to him:

♦ *All these I have observed; what do I still lack?*

Jesus said to him:

♦ *If you would be perfect, go, sell what you possess and give to the*

A SERIES OF JESUS' POWERFUL WORDS

poor, and you will have treasure in heaven; and come, follow me.

When the young man heard this he went away sorrowful; for he had great possessions.

(Matthew 19, 17 - 22; Mark 10, 19 - 22; Luke 18, 20 - 23)

The First and the Second Commandment

(The Sermon on the Mount)

ut when the Pharisees heard that he (Jesus) had silenced the Sadducees, they came together. And one of them, a lawyer, asked him a question, to test him.

♦ *Teacher, which is the great commandment in the law?*

And he said to him

♦ *You shall love the Lord your God with all your heart, and with all your soul, and with all your mind. This is the great and first commandment. And a second is like it, You shall love your neighbor as yourself. On these two commandments depend all the law and the prophets.*

(Matthew 22, 34 - 40; Mark 12; 30. 31; Luke 10, 27)

OVERCOME

In the World You Have Tribulation

Jesus (to his disciples):

n the world you have tribulation; but be of good cheer, I have overcome the world.

(John 16, 33)

THE TEACHINGS OF JESUS

PEACEMAKERS

Blessed Are the Peacemakers

(The Sermon on the Mount)

nd great crowds followed him (Jesus) from Galilee and the Decapolis and Jerusalem and Judea and from beyond the Jordan. Seeing the crowds, he went up on the mountain, and when he sat down his disciples came to him. And he opened his mouth and taught them, saying:

♦ *Blessed are the peacemakers, for they shall be called sons of God.*

(Matthew 4, 25; 5, 1. 2. 9)

PERFECT

If You Would Be Perfect, Go, Sell What You Possess and Give to the Poor

nd behold, one came up to him (Jesus), saying:

♦ *Teacher, what good deed must I do, to have eternal life?*

And he said to him:

♦ *Why do you ask me about what is good? One there is who is good. If you would enter life, keep the commandments.*

He said to him:

♦ *Which?*

And Jesus said:

♦ *You shall not kill, You shall not commit adultery, You shall not steal, You shall not bear false witness, Honor your father and mother, and, You shall love your neighbor as yourself.*

The young man said to him:

♦ *All these I have observed; what do I still lack?*

Jesus said to him:

♦ *If you would be perfect, go, sell what you possess and give to the poor, and you will have treasure in heaven; and come, follow me.*

When the young man heard this he went away sorrowful; for he had great possessions.

(Matthew 19, 16 - 22; Mark 10, 19 - 22; Luke 18, 20 - 23)

You Must Be Perfect, As Your Heavenly Father Is Perfect
(The Sermon on the Mount)

Jesus (to his disciples and the crowds):

You have heard that it was said, `You shall love your neighbor and hate your enemy.' But I say to you, Love your enemies and pray for those who persecute you, so that you may be sons of your Father who is in heaven; for he makes his sun rise on the evil and on the good, and sends rain on the just and on the unjust.

For if you love those who love you, what reward have you? Do not even the tax collectors do the same?

And if you salute only your brethren, what more are you doing than others? Do not even the Gentiles do the same?

THE TEACHINGS OF JESUS

You, therefore, must be perfect, as your heavenly Father is perfect.

(Matthew 5, 43 - 48; Luke 6, 27. 28. 32. 35. 36)

PERSECUTE

Blessed Are Those Who Are Persecuted for Righteousness' Sake
(The Sermon on the Mount)

nd great crowds followed him (Jesus) from Galilee and the Decapolis and Jerusalem and Judea and from beyond the Jordan. Seeing the crowds, he went up on the mountain, and when he sat down his disciples came to him. And he opened his mouth and taught them, saying:

♦ *Blessed are those who are persecuted for righteousness' sake, for theirs is the kingdom of heaven.*

(Matthew 4, 25; 5, 1. 2. 10)

Blessed Are You When Men Revile You and Persecute You on My Account
(The Sermon on the Mount)

nd great crowds followed him (Jesus) from Galilee and the Decapolis and Jerusalem and Judea and from beyond the Jordan. Seeing the crowds, he went up on the mountain, and when he sat down his disciples came to him. And he opened his mouth and taught them, saying:

♦ *Blessed are you when men revile you and persecute you and utter all kinds of evil against you falsely on my account.*

(Matthew 4, 25; 5, 1. 2. 11)

A SERIES OF JESUS' POWERFUL WORDS

The Hour Is Coming When Whoever Kills You Will Think He Is Offering Service to God

Jesus (to his disciples):

hey will put you out of the synagogues; indeed, the hour is coming when whoever kills you will think he is offering service to God. And they will do this because they have not known the Father, nor me.

(John 16, 2. 3)

If They Persecuted Me, They Will Persecute You

Jesus (to his disciples):

emember the word that I said to you, 'A servant is not greater than his master.' If they persecuted me, they will persecute you; if they kept my word, they will keep yours also. But all this they will do to you on my account, because they do not know him who sent me.

(John 15, 20. 21; Luke 6, 40; Matthew 10, 24; John 13, 16)

Your Reward Is Great in Heaven, for So Men Persecuted the Prophets Who Were Before You
(The Sermon on the Mount)

nd great crowds followed him (Jesus) from Galilee and the Decapolis and Jerusalem and Judea and from beyond the Jordan. Seeing the crowds, he went up on the mountain, and when he sat down his disciples came to him. And he opened his mouth and taught them, saying:

♦ *Rejoice and be glad, for your reward is great in heaven, for so men persecuted the prophets who were before you.*

(Matthew 4, 25; 5, 1. 2. 12)

PIETY

When You Give Alms, Do Not Let Your Left Hand Know What Your Right Hand Is Doing
(The Sermon on the Mount)

Jesus (to his disciples and the crowds):

eware of practicing your piety before men in order to be seen by them; for then you will have no reward from your Father who is in heaven. Thus, when you give alms, sound no trumpet before you, as the hypocrites do in the synagogues and in the streets, that they may be praised by men. Truly, I say to you, they have received their reward. But when you give alms, do not let your left hand know what your right hand is doing, so that your alms may be in secret; and your Father who sees in secret will reward you.

(Matthew 6, 1 - 4)

POOR

When You Give a Feast, Invite the Poor, the Maimed, the Lame, the Blind

ne sabbath when he (Jesus) went to dine at the house of a ruler who belonged to the Pharisees, they were watching him. He said also to the man who had invited him:

♦ *When you give a dinner or a banquet, do not invite your friends or your brothers or your kinsmen or rich neighbors, lest they also invite you in return, and you be repaid. But when you give a feast, invite the poor, the maimed, the lame, the blind, and you will be blessed, because they cannot repay you. You will be repaid at the resurrection of the just.*

(Luke 14, 1. 12 - 14)

POOR IN SPIRIT

Blessed Are the Poor in Spirit

(The Sermon on the Mount)

nd great crowds followed him (Jesus) from Galilee and the Decapolis and Jerusalem and Judea and from beyond the Jordan. Seeing the crowds, he went up on the mountain, and when he sat down his disciples came to him. And he opened his mouth and taught them, saying:

♦ *Blessed are the poor in spirit, for theirs is the kingdom of heaven.*

(Matthew 4, 25; 5, 3; Luke 6, 17 - 20)

POWER

You Will See the Son of Man Seated at the Right Hand of Power, and Coming on the Clouds of Heaven

ut Jesus was silent. And the high priest said to him:

♦ *I adjure you by the living God, tell us if you are the Christ, the Son of God.*

Jesus said to him:

♦ *You have said so. But I tell you, hereafter you will see the Son of man seated at the right hand of Power, and coming on the clouds of heaven.*

(Matthew 26, 63. 64, Luke 22, 67 - 69)

POWER OF CHRIST

My Power Is Made Perfect in Weakness

Paul (to Corinthians):

nd to keep me from being too elated by the abundance of revelations, a thorn was given me in the flesh, a messenger of Satan, to harass me, to keep me from being too elated. Three times I besought the Lord about this, that it should leave me; but he said to me:

➢ *My grace is sufficient for you, for my power is made perfect in weakness.*

♦ *I will all the more gladly boast of my weaknesses, that the power of Christ may rest upon me.*

(2. Corinthians 12, 7 - 9)

I Perceive That Power Has Gone Forth from Me

nd a woman who had had a flow of blood for twelve years and could not be healed by any one, came up behind him, and touched the fringe of his garment; and immediately her flow of blood ceased. And Jesus said:

♦ *Who was it that touched me?*

When all denied it, Peter said:

♦ *Master, the multitudes surround you and press upon you!*

But Jesus said:

♦ *Some one touched me; for I perceive that power has gone forth from me.*

And when the woman saw that she was not hidden, she came trembling, and falling down before him declared in the presence of all the people why she had touched him, and how she had been immediately healed. And he said to her:

Daughter, your faith has made you well; go in peace.

(Luke 8, 43 - 48; Mark 5, 25 - 34)

For with Authority and Power He Commands the Unclean Spirits?

nd he (Jesus) went down to Capernaum, a city of Galilee. And he was teaching them on the sabbath; and they were astonished at his teaching, for his word was with authority. And in the synagogue there was a man who had the spirit of an unclean demon; and he cried out with a loud voice:

♦ *Ah! What have you to do with us, Jesus of Nazareth? Have you come to destroy us? I know who you are, the Holy One of God.*

But Jesus rebuked him, saying:

♦ *Be silent, and come out of him!*

And when the demon had thrown him down in the midst, he came out of him, having done him no harm. And they were all amazed and said to one another:

THE TEACHINGS OF JESUS

♦ *What is this word? For with authority and power he commands the unclean spirits, and they come out.*

And reports of him went out into every place in the surrounding region.

(Luke 4, 31 - 37)

All the Crowd Sought To Touch Him, for Power Came Forth from Him and Healed Them All

(The Sermon on the Mount)

nd he (Jesus) came down with them and stood on a level place, with a great crowd of his disciples and a great multitude of people from all Judea and Jerusalem and the seacoast of Tyre and Sidon, who came to hear him and to be healed of their diseases; and those who were troubled with unclean spirits were cured. And all the crowd sought to touch him, for power came forth from him and healed them all.

(Luke 6, 17 - 19)

They Will See the Son of Man Coming on the Clouds of Heaven with Power and Great Glory

Jesus (to his disciples):

*or as the lightning comes from the east and shines as far as the west, so will be the coming of the Son of man. Wherever the body is, there the eagles will be gathered together.*

Immediately after the tribulation of those days the sun will be darkened, and the moon will not give its light, and the stars will

fall from heaven, and the powers of the heavens will be shaken; then will appear the sign of the Son of man in heaven, and then all the tribes of the earth will mourn, and they will see the Son of man coming on the clouds of heaven with power and great glory; and he will send out his angels with a loud trumpet call, and they will gather his elect from the four winds, from one end of heaven to the other.

(Matthew 24, 27 - 31; Mark 13, 24 - 27)

Power and Authority over All Demons

nd he (Jesus) called the twelve together and gave them power and authority over all demons and to cure diseases, and he sent them out to preach the kingdom of God and to heal. And he said to them:

♦ *Take nothing for your journey, no staff, nor bag, nor bread, nor money; and do not have two tunics. And whatever house you enter, stay there, and from there depart. And wherever they do not receive you, when you leave that town shake off the dust from your feet as a testimony against them.*

And they departed and went through the villages, preaching the gospel and healing everywhere.

(Luke 9, 1 - 6)

PRAY

Always to Pray and Not Lose Heart

nd he (Jesus) told them a parable, to the effect that they ought always to pray and not lose heart. He said:

♦ *In a certain city there was a judge who neither feared God* *nor regarded man; and there was a widow in that city who kept coming to him and saying, `Vindicate me against my adversary.' For a while he refused; but afterward he said to himself, `Though I neither fear God nor regard man, yet because this widow bothers me, I will vindicate her, or she will wear me out by her continual coming.'*

And the Lord said:

♦ *Hear what the unrighteous judge says. And will not God vindicate his elect, who cry to him day and night? Will he delay long over them? I tell you, he will vindicate them speedily.*

Nevertheless, when the Son of man comes, will he find faith on earth?

(Luke 18, 1 - 8)

Watch and Pray That You May Not Enter into Temptation

Jesus (to Peter, James and John):

atch and pray that you may not enter into temptation; the spirit indeed is willing, but the flesh is weak.

(Matthew 26, 41; Mark 14, 38; Luke 22, 46)

This Kind Cannot Be Driven Out by Anything but Prayer

nd when he (Jesus) had entered the house, his disciples asked him privately:

♦ *Why could we not cast it out?*

And he said to them:

♦ *This kind cannot be driven out by anything but prayer.*

(Mark 9, 28. 29)

When You Pray, You Must Not Be Like the Hypocrites
(The Sermon on the Mount)

Jesus (to his disciples and the crowds):

nd when you pray, you must not be like the hypocrites; for they love to stand and pray in the synagogues and at the street corners, that they may be seen by men. Truly, I say to you, they have received their reward. But when you pray, go into your room and shut the door and pray to your Father who is in secret; and your Father who sees in secret will reward you. And in praying do not heap up empty phrases as the Gentiles do; for they think that they will be heard for their many words. Do not be like them, for your Father knows what you need before you ask him.

(Matthew 6, 5 - 8)

Our Father
(The Sermon on the Mount)

Jesus (to his disciples and the crowds):

ray then like this:

Our Father who art in heaven,
Hallowed be thy name.
Thy kingdom come
Thy will be done,

THE TEACHINGS OF JESUS

On earth as it is in heaven.
Give us this day our daily bread;
And forgive us our debts,
As we also have forgiven our debtors;
And lead us not into temptation,
But deliver us from evil.

(Matthew 6, 9 - 13; Luke 11, 1 - 4)

Watch at All Times, Praying That You May Have Strength to Escape All These Things

Jesus (to his disciples):

ut take heed to yourselves lest your hearts be weighed down with dissipation and drunkenness and cares of this life, and that day come upon you suddenly like a snare; for it will come upon all who dwell upon the face of the whole earth.

But watch at all times, praying that you may have strength to escape all these things that will take place, and to stand before the Son of man.

(Luke 21, 34 - 36; Matthew 24, 42; 25, 13; Mark 13, 33)

PRIDE

Out of the Heart of Man, Come Evil Thoughts

nd he (Jesus) called the people to him again, and said to them:

♦ *Hear me, all of you, and understand: there is nothing outside a man which by going into him can defile him; but the things which come out of a man are what defile him.*

And when he had entered the house, and left the people, his disciples asked him about the parable. And he said to them:

♦ *Then are you also without understanding? Do you not see that whatever goes into a man from outside cannot defile him, since it enters, not his heart but his stomach, and so passes on?*

(Thus he declared all foods clean.)

And he said:

♦ *What comes out of a man is what defiles a man. For from within, out of the heart of man, come evil thoughts, fornication, theft, murder, adultery, coveting, wickedness, deceit, licentiousness, envy, slander, pride, foolishness. All these evil things come from within, and they defile a man.*

(Mark 7, 14 - 23;   Matthew 15, 10 - 20)

PROCLAIM

Leave the Dead to Bury Their Own Dead, but You Go and Proclaim the Kingdom of God

s they (Jesus and his disciples) were going along the road, a man said to him:

♦ *I will follow you wherever you go.*

And Jesus said to him:

♦ *Foxes have holes, and birds of the air have nests; but the Son of man has nowhere to lay his head.*

To another he said:

♦ *Follow me.*

But he said:

♦ *Lord, let me first go and bury my father.*

But he said to him:

♦ *Leave the dead to bury their own dead; but as for you, go and proclaim the kingdom of God.*

Another said:

♦ *I will follow you, Lord; but let me first say farewell to those at my home.*

Jesus said to him:

♦ *No one who puts his hand to the plow and looks back is fit for the kingdom of God.*

(Luke 9, 57 - 62)

PROPHETS

Take Heed That No One Leads You Astray

As he (Jesus) sat on the Mount of Olives, the disciples came to him privately, saying:

♦ *Tell us, when will this be, and what will be the sign of your coming and of the close of the age?*

And Jesus answered them:

♦ *Take heed that no one leads you astray. For many will come in my name, saying, `I am the Christ,' and they will lead many astray.*

(Matthew 24, 3 - 5. 11; Mark 13, 3 - 6; Luke 21, 7. 8)

A SERIES OF JESUS' POWERFUL WORDS

Beware of False Prophets
(The Sermon on the Mount)

Jesus (to his disciples and the crowds):

eware of false prophets, who come to you in sheep's clothing but inwardly are ravenous wolves. You will know them by their fruits. Are grapes gathered from thorns, or figs from thistles? So, every sound tree bears good fruit, but the bad tree bears evil fruit. A sound tree cannot bear evil fruit, nor can a bad tree bear good fruit. Every tree that does not bear good fruit is cut down and thrown into the fire. Thus you will know them by their fruits.

(Matthew 7, 15 - 20)

Whatever You Wish That Men Would Do to You, Do So to Them
(The Sermon on the Mount)

Jesus (to his disciples and the crowds):

o whatever you wish that men would do to you, do so to them; for this is the law and the prophets.

(Matthew 7, 12; Luke 6, 31)

All the Prophets and the Law Prophesied Until John

s they (two disciples of John the Baptist) went away, Jesus began to speak to the crowds concerning John:

♦ *What did you go out into the wilderness to behold? A reed shaken by the wind? From the days of John the Bap-*

tist until now the kingdom of heaven has suffered violence, and men of violence take it by force. For all the prophets and the law prophesied until John; and if you are willing to accept it, he is Elijah who is to come.

(Matthew 11, 7. 12. 13; Luke 16, 16)

I Have Come Not to Abolish the Law and the Prophets
(The Sermon on the Mount)

Jesus (to his disciples and the crowds):

hink not that I have come to abolish the law and the prophets; I have come not to abolish them but to fulfil them. For truly, I say to you, till heaven and earth pass away, not an iota, not a dot, will pass from the law until all is accomplished.

(Matthew 5, 17. 18; Luke 16, 17)

On the First and Second Commandment Depend All the Law and the Prophets
(The Sermon on the Mount)

Jesus (to the rich young man):

ou shall love the Lord your God with all your heart, and with all your soul, and with all your mind. This is the great and first commandment. And a second is like it, You shall love your neighbor as yourself. On these two commandments depend all the law and the prophets.

(Matthew 22, 37 - 40; Mark 12; 30. 31; Luke 10, 27)

A SERIES OF JESUS' POWERFUL WORDS

Woe to You, When All Men Speak Well of You
(The Sermon on the Mount)

Jesus (to his disciples and a great multitude
 of people from all Judea and Jerusalem
 and the seacost of Tyre and Sidon):

oe to you, when all men speak well of you, for so their fathers did to the false prophets.

(Luke 6, 26)

PURE IN HEART
Blessed Are the Pure in Heart
(The Sermon on the Mount)

nd great crowds followed him (Jesus) from Galilee and the Decapolis and Jerusalem and Judea and from beyond the Jordan. Seeing the crowds, he went up on the mountain, and when he sat down his disciples came to him. And he opened his mouth and taught them, saying:

♦ *Blessed are the pure in heart, for they shall see God.*

(Matthew 4, 25; 5, 1. 2. 8)

RAISE UP
I Will Raise Him Up at the Last Day

Jesus (to the Jews):

o one can come to me unless the Father who sent me draws him; and I will raise him up at the last day.

(John 6, 44)

THE TEACHINGS OF JESUS

He Who Eats My Flesh and Drinks My Blood
I Will Raise Him Up at the Last Day

Jesus (to the Jews):

ruly, truly, I say to you, unless you eat the flesh of the Son of man and drink his blood, you have no life in you; he who eats my flesh and drinks my blood has eternal life, and I will raise him up at the last day. For my flesh is foo indeed, and my blood is drink indeed.

(John 6, 53 - 55)

READY

You Also Must Be Ready

Jesus (to his disciples and the crowds):

et your loins be girded and your lamps burning, and be like men who are waiting for their master to come home from the marriage feast, so that they may open to him at once when he comes and knocks.

Blessed are those servants whom the master finds awake when he comes; truly, I say to you, he will gird himself and have them sit at table, and he will come and serve them. If he comes in the second watch, or in the third, and finds them so, blessed are those servants! But know this, that if the householder had known at what hour the thief was coming, he would not have left his house to be broken into.

You also must be ready; for the Son of man is coming at an unexpected hour.

(Luke 12, 35 - 40; Matthew 24, 43. 44)

A SERIES OF JESUS' POWERFUL WORDS

REBUKE

If Your Brother Sins, Rebuke Him, and If He Repents, Forgive Him

Jesus (to his disciples):

ake heed to yourselves; if your brother sins, rebuke him, and if he repents, forgive him; and if he sins against you seven times in the day, and turns to you seven times, and says, `I repent,' you must forgive him.

(Luke 17, 3. 4)

RECEIVE

It Is More Blessed to Give

Jesus (to his disciples):

t is more blessed to give than to receive.

(Acts 20, 35)

RECONCILED

First Be Reconciled to Your Brother, and Then Come and Offer Your Gift

(The Sermon on the Mount)

Jesus (to his disciples and the crowds):

o if you are offering your gift at the altar, and there remember that your brother has something against you, leave your gift there before the altar and go; first be reconciled to your brother, and then come and offer your gift. Make friends quickly with your accuser, while you are going with him to court,

lest your accuser hand you over to the judge, and the judge to the guard, and you be put in prison; truly, I say to you, you will never get out till you have paid the last penny.

(Matthew 5, 23 - 26; Luke 12, 58. 59)

RENOUNCE

Whoever of You Does Not Renounce All That He Has Cannot Be My Disciple
(The Sermon on the Mount)

ow great multitudes accompanied him (Jesus); and he turned and said to them:

♦ *If any one comes to me and does not hate his own father and mother and wife and children and brothers and sisters, yes, and even his own life, he cannot be my disciple. Whoever does not bear his own cross and come after me, cannot be my disciple.*

For which of you, desiring to build a tower, does not first sit down and count the cost, whether he has enough to complete it? Otherwise, when he has laid a foundation, and is not able to finish, all who see it begin to mock him, saying, `This man began to build, and was not able to finish.'

Or what king, going to encounter another king in war, will not sit down first and take counsel whether he is able with ten thousand to meet him who comes against him with twenty thousand? And if not, while the other is yet a great way off, he sends an embassy and asks terms of peace. So therefore, whoever of you does not renounce all that he has cannot be my disciple.

(Luke 14, 25 - 33; 9, 23; Matthew 10, 37;   16, 24;   Mark 8, 34. 35)

A SERIES OF JESUS' POWERFUL WORDS

If You Would Be Perfect, Go, Sell What You Possess and Give to the Poor

nd behold, one came up to him (Jesus), saying:

♦ *Teacher, what good deed must I do, to have eternal life?*

And he said to him:

♦ *Why do you ask me about what is good? One there is who is good. If you would enter life, keep the commandments.*

He said to him:

♦ *Which?*

And Jesus said:

♦ *You shall not kill, You shall not commit adultery, You shall not steal, You shall not bear false witness, Honor your father and mother, and, You shall love your neighbor as yourself.*

The young man said to him:

♦ *All these I have observed; what do I still lack?*

Jesus said to him:

♦ *If you would be perfect, go, sell what you possess and give to the poor, and you will have treasure in heaven; and come, follow me.*

When the young man heard this he went away sorrowful; for he had great possessions. And Jesus said to his disciples:

♦ *Truly, I say to you, it will be hard for a rich man to enter the kingdom of heaven.*

(Matthew 19, 16 - 22;   Mark 10, 19 - 22;   Luke 18, 20 - 23)

THE TEACHINGS OF JESUS

REPENT

Joy in Heaven over One Sinner Who Repents

Jesus (to Pharisees and scribes):

hat man of you, having a hundred sheep, if he has lost one of them, does not leave the ninety-nine in the wilderness, and go after the one which is lost, until he finds it? And when he has found it, he lays it on his shoulders, rejoicing. And when he comes home, he calls together his friends and his neighbors, saying to them, `Rejoice with me, for I have found my sheep which was lost.'

Just so, I tell you, there will be more joy in heaven over one sinner who repents than over ninety-nine righteous per-sons who need no repentance.

(Luke 15, 4 - 7)

Woe to You, Chorazin, Bethsaida and Capernaum

hen he (Jesus) began to upbraid the cities where most of his mighty works had been done, because they did not repent:

♦ *Woe to you, Chorazin! woe to you, Bethsaida! for if the the mighty works done in you had been done in Tyre and Sidon, they would have repented long ago in sackcloth and ashes.*

But I tell you, it shall be more tolerable on the day of judgment for Tyre and Sidon than for you. And you, Capernaum, will you be exalted to heaven? You shall be brought down to Hades. For if the mighty works done in you had been done in Sodom, it would have remained until this day.

But I tell you that it shall be more tolerable on the day of judgment for the land of Sodom than for you.

(Matthew 11, 20 - 24; Luke 10, 13. 14)

If Your Brother Sins, Rebuke Him, and if He Repents, Forgive Him

Jesus (to his disciples):

ake heed to yourselves; if your brother sins, rebuke him, and if he repents, forgive him; and if he sins against you seven times in the day, and turns to you seven times, and says, `I repent,' you must forgive him.

(Luke 17, 3. 4)

Unless You Repent You Will All Likewise Perish

here were some present at that very time who told him (Jesus) of the Galileans whose blood Pilate had mingled with their sacrifices. And he answered them:

♦ *Do you think that these Galileans were worse sinners than all the other Galileans, because they suffered thus? I tell you, No; but unless you repent you will all likewise perish. Or those eighteen upon whom the tower in Siloam fell and killed them, do you think that they were worse offenders than all the others who dwelt in Jerusalem?*

I tell you, No; but unless you repent you will all like-wise perish.

(Luke 13, 1 - 5)

I Came Not to Call the Righteous, but Sinners

Jesus (to the Pharisees):

hose who are well have no need of a physician, but those who are sick. Go and learn what this means, `I desire mercy, and not sacrifice.' For I came not to call the righteous, but sinners.

(Matthew 9, 12. 13)

Repent, for the Kingdom of Heaven Is at Hand

n those days came John the Baptist, preaching in the wilderness of Judea:

♦ *Repent, for the kingdom of heaven is at hand.*

(Matthew 3, 1. 2)

RESIST

Do Not Resist One Who Is Evil

(The Sermon on the Mount)

Jesus (to his disciples and the crowds):

ou have heard that it was said, `An eye for an eye and a tooth for a tooth.' But I say to you, Do not resist one who is evil. But if any one strikes you on the right cheek, turn to him the other also; and if any one would sue you and take your coat, let him have your cloak as well; and if any one forces you to go one mile, go with him two miles.

(Matthew 5, 38 - 41; Luke 6, 29)

REST

You Will Find Rest for Your Souls

Jesus (to his disciples and the crowds):

 *ome to me, all who labor and are heavy laden, and I will give you rest. Take my yoke upon you, and learn from me; for I am gentle and lowly in heart, and you will find rest for your souls. For my yoke is easy, and my burden is light.*

(Matthew 11, 28 - 30)

RESURRECTION

I Am the Resurrection and the Life

Jesus (to Martha):

 *am the resurrection and the life; he who believes in me, though he die, yet shall he live, and whoever lives and believes in me shall never die.*

(John 11, 25. 26)

RESURRECTION OF LIFE

Those Who Have Done Good, Come Forth to the Resurrection of Life

Jesus (to the Jews):

 *o not marvel at this; for the hour is coming when all who are in the tombs will hear his voice and come forth, those who have done good, to the resurrection of life, and those who have done evil, to the resurrection of judgment.*

(John 5, 28. 29)

THE TEACHINGS OF JESUS

RETURN

What Shall a Man Give in
Return for His Life

Jesus (to his disciples):

or what will it profit a man, if he gains the whole world and forfeits his life? Or what shall a man give in return for his life?

(Matthew 16, 26; Mark 8, 36. 37; Luke 9, 25)

REVEALED

Nothing Is Covered That Will
Not Be Revealed

Jesus (to his disciples):

o have no fear of them; for nothing is covered that will not be revealed, or hidden that will not be known. What I tell you in the dark, utter in the light; and what you hear whispered, proclaim upon the housetops.

(Matthew 10, 26. 27; Mark 4, 22; Luke 8, 17; 12, 21. 3)

REVILE

Blessed Are You When
Men Revile You

(The Sermon on the Mount)

nd great crowds followed him (Jesus) from Galilee and the Decapolis and Jerusalem and Judea and from beyond the Jordan. Seeing the crowds, he went up on the mountain, and when he sat down his disciples came to him. And he opened his mouth and taught them, saying:

♦ *Blessed are you when men revile you and persecute you and utter all kinds of evil against you falsely on my account.*

(Matthew 4, 25; 5, 1. 2. 11; Luke 6, 17 - 20. 22)

REWARD

Your Father Who Sees in Secret Will Reward You
(The Sermon on the Mount)

Jesus (to his disciples and the crowds):

hen you give alms, do not let your left hand know what your right hand is doing, so that your alms may be in secret; and your Father who sees in secret will reward you.

(Matthew 6, 3. 4)

Every One Who Has Left All, for My Name's Sake, Will Receive a Hundredfold, and Inherit Eternal Life

Peter (to Jesus):

o, we have left everything and followed you. What then shall we have?

Jesus said to them:

♦ *Truly, I say to you, in the new world, when the Son of man shall sit on his glorious throne, you who have followed me will also sit on twelve thrones, judging the twelve tribes of Israel. And every one who has left houses or brothers or sisters or father or mother or children or lands, for my name's sake, will receive a hundred-*

fold, and inherit eternal life. But many that are first will be last, and the last first.

(Matthew 19, 27 - 30; Mark 10, 28 - 31; Luke 18, 28 - 30; 22, 30)

RICH MAN

Woe to You That Are Rich
(The Sermon on the Mount)

Jesus (to his disciples and a great multitude
of people from all Judea and Jerusalem
and the seacost of Tyre and Sidon):

ut woe to you that are rich, for you have received your consolation.

(Luke 6, 24)

It Will Be Hard for a Rich Man to Enter the Kingdom of Heaven

Jesus (to his disciples):

ruly, I say to you, it will be hard for a rich man to enter the kingdom of heaven. Again I tell you, it is easier for a camel to go through the eye of a needle than for a rich man to enter the kingdom of God.

When the disciples heard this they were greatly astonished, saying:

♦ *Who then can be saved?*

But Jesus looked at them and said to them:

With men this is impossible, but with God all things are possible.

(Matthew 19, 23 - 26; Mark 10, 23 - 27; Luke 18, 24 - 27)

A SERIES OF JESUS' POWERFUL WORDS

RIGHTEOUS

I Came Not to Call the Righteous, but Sinners

Jesus (to the Pharisees):

hose who are well have no need of a physician, but those who are sick. Go and learn what this means, 'I desire mercy, and not sacrifice.' For I came not to call the righteous, but sinners.

(Matthew 9, 12. 13)

Seek First the Kingdom of God and His Righteousness

(The Sermon on the Mount)

Jesus (to his disciples and the crowds):

herefore I tell you, do not be anxious about your life, what you shall eat or what you shall drink, nor about your body, what you shall put on. Is not life more than food, and the body more than clothing?

Look at the birds of the air: they neither sow nor reap nor gather into barns, and yet your heavenly Father feeds them. Are you not of more value than they?

And which of you by being anxious can add one cubit to his span of life?

And why are you anxious about clothing? Consider the lilies of the field, how they grow; they neither toil nor spin; yet I tell you, even Solomon in all his glory was not arrayed like one of these.

But if God so clothes the grass of the field, which today is alive and tomorrow is thrown into the oven, will he not much more clothe you, O men of little faith?

Therefore do not be anxious, saying, `What shall we eat?' or ` What shall we drink?' or `What shall we wear?' For the Gentiles seek all these things; and your heavenly Father knows that you need them all. But seek first his kingdom and his righteousness, and all these things shall be yours as well.

Therefore do not be anxious about tomorrow, for tomorrow will be anxious for itself. Let the day's own trouble be sufficient for the day.

(Matthew 6, 25 - 34; Luke 12, 22 - 31)

The Counselor Will Convince the World Concerning Sin and Righteousness and Judgment

Jesus (to his disciples):

evertheless I tell you the truth: it is to your advantage that I go away, for if I do not go away, the Counselor will not come to you; but if I go, I will send him to you. And when he comes, he will convince the world concerning sin and righteousness and judgment: concerning sin, because they do not believe in me; concerning righteousness, because I go to the Father, and you will see me no more; concerning judgment, because the ruler of this world is judged.

I have yet many things to say to you, but you cannot bear them now. When the Spirit of truth comes, he will guide you into all the truth; for he will not speak on his own authority, but whatever he hears he

A SERIES OF JESUS' POWERFUL WORDS

will speak, and he will declare to you the things that are to come. He will glorify me, for he will take what is mine and declare it to you. All that the Father has is mine; therefore I said that he will take what is mine and declare it to you.

(John 16, 7 - 15)

Blessed Are Those Who Hunger and Thirst for Righteousness
(The Sermon on the Mount)

nd great crowds followed him (Jesus) from Galilee and the Decapolis and Jerusalem and Judea and from beyond the Jordan. Seeing the crowds, he went up on the mountain, and when he sat down his disciples came to him. And he opened his mouth and taught them, saying:

♦ *Blessed are those who hunger and thirst for righteousness, for they shall be satisfied.*

(Matthew 4, 25; 5, 1. 2. 6; Luke 6, 17 - 21)

Blessed Are Those Who Are Persecuted for Righteousness' Sake
(The Sermon on the Mount)

nd great crowds followed him (Jesus) from Galilee and the Decapolis and Jerusalem and Judea and from beyond the Jordan. Seeing the crowds, he went up on the mountain, and when he sat down his disciples came to him. And he opened his mouth and taught them, saying:

♦ *Blessed are those who are persecuted for righteousness' sake, for theirs is the kingdom of heaven.*

(Matthew 4, 25; 5, 1. 2. 10)

Your Righteousness Must Exceed That of the Scribes and Pharisees

(The Sermon on the Mount)

Jesus (to his disciples and the crowds):

or I tell you, unless your righteousness exceeds that of the scribes and Pharisees, you will never enter the kingdom of heaven.

(Matthew 5, 20)

RULER OF THIS WORLD

Now Shall the Ruler of This World Be Cast Out

Jesus (to his Father):

ow is my soul troubled. And what shall I say? `Father, save me from this hour'? No, for this purpose I have come to this hour. Father, glorify thy name.

Then a voice came from heaven:

➢ *I have glorified it, and I will glorify it again.*

The crowd standing by heard it and said that it had thundered. Others said:

♦ *An angel has spoken to him.*

Jesus answered:

♦ *This voice has come for your sake, not for mine. Now is the judgment of this world, now shall the ruler of this world be cast out.*

(John 12, 28 - 31)

A SERIES OF JESUS' POWERFUL WORDS

The Ruler of This World Is Judged

Jesus (to his disciples):

evertheless I tell you the truth: it is to your advantage that I go away, for if I do not go away, the Counselor will not come to you; but if I go, I will send him to you. And when he comes, he will convince the world concerning sin and righteousness and judgment: concerning sin, because they do not believe in me; concerning righteousness, because I go to the Father, and you will see me no more; concerning judgment, because the ruler of this world is judged.

(John 16, 7 - 11)

SABBATH

Loosing from Satan's Bond on the Sabbath Day

ut the ruler of the synagogue, indignant because Jesus had healed on the sabbath, said to the people:

♦ *There are six days on which work ought to be done; come on those days and be healed, and not on the sabbath day.*

Then the Lord answered him:

♦ *You hypocrites! Does not each of you on the sabbath untie his ox or his ass from the manger, and lead it away to water it? And ought not this woman, a daughter of Abraham whom Satan bound for eighteen years, be loosed from this bond on the sabbath day?*

As he said this, all his adversaries were put to shame; and all the people rejoiced at all the glorious things that were done by him.

(Luke 13, 14 - 17)

The Son of Man Is Lord Even of the Sabbath

Jesus (to the Pharisees):

ne sabbath he was going through the grainfields; and as they made their way his disciples began to pluck heads of grain. And the Pharisees said to him:

♦ *Look, why are they doing what is not lawful on the sabbath?*

And he said to them:

♦ *Have you never read what David did, when he was in need and was hungry, he and those who were with him: how he entered the house of God, when Abiathar was high priest, and ate the bread of the Presence, which it is not lawful for any but the priests to eat, and also gave it to those who were with him?*

And he said to them:

♦ *The sabbath was made for man, not man for the sabbath; so the Son of man is lord even of the sabbath.*

(Mark 2, 23 - 28; Matthew 12, 1 - 8)

SACRIFICE

Go and Learn What This Means, `I Desire Mercy, and Not Sacrifice`

nd as he (Jesus) sat at table in the house, behold, many tax collectors and sinners came and sat down with Jesus and his disciples. And when the Pharisees saw this, they said to his disciples:

♦ *Why does your teacher eat with tax collectors and sinners?*

A SERIES OF JESUS' POWERFUL WORDS

But when he heard it, he said:

♦ *Those who are well have no need of a physician, but those who are sick. Go and learn what this means, `I desire mercy, and not sacrifice.' For I came not to call the righteous, but sinners.*

(Matthew 9, 10 - 13)

I Desire Mercy, and Not Sacrifice

Jesus (to the Pharisees):

nd if you had known what this means, `I desire mercy, and not sacrifice,' you would not have condemned the guiltless.

(Matthew 12, 7)

SALT

You Are the Salt of the Earth

(The Sermon on the Mount)

nd great crowds followed him (Jesus) from Galilee and the Decapolis and Jerusalem and Judea and from beyond the Jordan. Seeing the crowds, he went up on the mountain, and when he sat down his disciples came to him. And he opened his mouth and taught them, saying:

♦ *You are the salt of the earth; but if salt has lost its taste, how shall its saltness be restored? It is no longer good for anything except to be thrown out and trodden under foot by men.*

(Matthew 4, 25; 5, 1. 2. 13; Mark 9, 50; Luke 14, 34. 35)

SATAN

The Ruler of This World Is Judged

Jesus (to his disciples):

evertheless I tell you the truth: it is to your advantage that I go away, for if I do not go away, the Counselor will not come to you; but if I go, I will send him to you. And when he comes, he will convince the world concerning sin and righteousness and judgment: concerning sin, because they do not believe in me; concerning righteousness, because I go to the Father, and you will see me no more; concerning judgment, because the ruler of this world is judged.

(John 16, 7 - 11)

Now Shall the Ruler of This World Be Cast Out

Jesus (to his disciples and the crowds):

ow is the judgment of this world, now shall the ruler of this world be cast out; and I, when I am lifted up from the earth, will draw all men to myself.

(John 12, 31. 32)

Jesus Loosed a Daughter of Abraham from Bond on the Sabbath Day

ut the ruler of the synagogue, indignant because Jesus had healed on the sabbath, said to the people:

♦ *There are six days on which work ought to be done; come on those days and be healed, and not on the sabbath day.*

A SERIES OF JESUS' POWERFUL WORDS

Then the Lord answered him:

♦ *You hypocrites! Does not each of you on the sabbath untie his ox or his ass from the manger, and lead it away to water it? And ought not this woman, a daughter of Abraham whom Satan bound for eighteen years, be loosed from this bond on the sabbath day?*

As he said this, all his adversaries were put to shame; and all the people rejoiced at all the glorious things that were done by him.

(Luke 13, 14 - 17)

Satan Fall from Heaven

Jesus (to the seventy):

saw Satan fall like lightning from heaven.

(Luke 10, 18)

SAVED

He Who Believes and Is Baptized Will Be Saved

Jesus (to the eleven):

o into all the world and preach the gospel to the whole creation. He who believes and is baptized will be saved; but he who does not believe will be condemned. And these signs will accompany those who believe: in my name they will cast out demons; they will speak in new tongues; they will pick up serpents, and if they drink any deadly thing, it will not hurt them; they will lay their hands on the sick, and they will recover.

(Mark 16, 15 - 18; Luke 10, 19)

THE TEACHINGS OF JESUS

Who Then Can Be Saved?

Jesus (to his disciples):

ruly, I say to you, it will be hard for a rich man to enter the kingdom of heaven. Again I tell you, it is easier for a camel to go through the eye of a needle than for a rich man to enter the kingdom of God.

When the disciples heard this they were greatly astonished, saying:

♦ *Who then can be saved?*

But Jesus looked at them and said to them:

♦ *With men this is impossible, but with God all things are possible.*

(Matthew 19, 23 - 26; Mark 10, 23 - 27; Luke 18, 24 - 27)

Gaining Your Lives

Jesus (to his disciples):

y your endurance you will gain your lives.

(Luke 21, 19; Matthew 24, 13)

SAVIOR

I Did Not Come to Judge the World but to Save the World

Jesus (to his disciples and the crowds):

e who believes in me, believes not in me but in him who sent me. And he who sees me sees him who sent me. I have come as light into the world, that whoever believes in me may not

remain in darkness. If any one hears my sayings and does not keep them, I do not judge him; for I did not come to judge the world but to save the world.

(John 12, 44 - 47)

SEEK

Every One Who Asks Receives, and He Who Seeks Finds, and to Him Who Knocks It Will Be Opened

(The Sermon on the Mount)

Jesus (to his disciples and the crowds):

sk, and it will be given you; seek, and you will find; knock, and it will be opened to you. For every one who asks receives, and he who seeks finds, and to him who knocks it will be opened.

Or what man of you, if his son asks him for bread, will give him a stone? Or if he asks for a fish, will give him a serpent? If you then, who are evil, know how to give good gifts to your children, how much more will your Father who is in heaven give good things to those who ask him!

(Matthew 7, 7 - 11; Luke 11, 9 - 13)

Seek First the Kingdom of God and His Righteousness

Jesus (to his disciples and the crowds):

herefore I tell you, do not be anxious about your life, what you shall eat or what you shall drink, nor about your body, what you shall put on. Is not life more than food, and the

THE TEACHINGS OF JESUS

body more than clothing?

Look at the birds of the air: they neither sow nor reap nor gather into barns, and yet your heavenly Father feeds them. Are you not of more value than they?

And which of you by being anxious can add one cubit to his span of life?

And why are you anxious about clothing? Consider the lilies of the field, how they grow; they neither toil nor spin; yet I tell you, even Solomon in all his glory was not arrayed like one of these. But if God so clothes the grass of the field, which today is alive and tomorrow is thrown into the oven, will he not much more clothe you, O men of little faith?

Therefore do not be anxious, saying, `What shall we eat?' or ` What shall we drink?' or `What shall we wear?' For the Gentiles seek all these things; and your heavenly Father knows that you need them all. But seek first his kingdom and his righteousness, and all these things shall be yours as well. Therefore do not be anxious about tomorrow, for tomorrow will be anxious for itself. Let the day's own trouble be sufficient for the day.

(Matthew 6, 25 - 34; Luke 12, 22 - 31)

SERPENTS

Be Wise As Serpents and Innocent As Doves

Jesus (to his disciples):

*ehold, I send you out as sheep in the midst of wolves; so be wise as serpents and innocent as doves. Beware of men; for they will deliver you up to councils, and flog you in*

their synagogues, and you will be dragged before governors and kings for my sake, to bear testimony before them and the Gentiles. When they deliver you up, do not be anxious how you are to speak or what you are to say; for what you are to say will be given to you in that hour; for it is not you who speak, but the Spirit of your Father speaking through you.

(Matthew 10, 16 - 20; Luke 10, 3)

SERVANT

Must Be Last of All and Servant

Jesus (to his disciples):

If any one would be first, he must be last of all and servant of all.

(Mark 9, 35)

A Servant Is Not Greater Than His Master

When he (Jesus) had washed their feet, and taken his garments, and resumed his place, he said to them:

♦ *Do you know what I have done to you? You call me Teacher and Lord; and you are right, for so I am. If I then, your Lord and Teacher, have washed your feet, you also ought to wash one another's feet. For I have given you an example, that you also should do as I have done to you. Truly, truly, I say to you, a servant is not greater than his master; nor is he who is sent greater than he who sent him. If you know these things, blessed are you if you do them.*

(John 13, 12 - 17)

THE TEACHINGS OF JESUS

Who Is Greatest Among You Shall Be Your Servant

Jesus (to his disciples):

e who is greatest among you shall be your servant; whoever exalts himself will be humbled, and whoever humbles himself will be exalted.

(Matthew 23, 11. 12;   Luke 14, 11;   18, 14)

Unworthy Servants

Jesus (to his disciples):

ill any one of you, who has a servant plowing or keeping sheep, say to him when he has come in from the field, `Come at once and sit down at table'?

Will he not rather say to him, `Prepare supper for me, and gird yourself and serve me, till I eat and drink; and afterward you shall eat and drink'? Does he thank the servant because he did what was commanded?

So you also, when you have done all that is commanded you, say, `We are unworthy servants; we have only done what was our duty.

(Luke 17, 7 - 10)

Whoever Would Be Great Among You Must Be Your Servant

nd when the ten heard it (the mother of the sons of Zebedee asked Jesus: "Command that these two sons of mine may sit, one at your right hand and one at your left, in your kingdom") they were indignant at the two brothers. But

A SERIES OF JESUS' POWERFUL WORDS

Jesus called them to him and said:

♦ *You know that the rulers of the Gentiles lord it over them, and their great men exercise authority over them. It shall not be so among you; but whoever would be great among you must be your servant, and whoever would be first among you must be your slave; even as the Son of man came not to be served but to serve, and to give his life as a ransom for many.*

(Matthew 20, 24 - 28; Mark 9, 35; 10, 41 - 45; Luke 22, 24 - 26)

I Am Among You As One Who Serves

Jesus (to his disciples):

or which is the greater, one who sits at table, or one who serves? Is it not the one who sits at table? But I am among you as one who serves. You are those who have continued with me in my trials; and I assign to you, as my Father assigned to me, a kingdom, that you may eat and drink at my table in my kingdom, and sit on thrones judging the twelve tribes of Israel.

(Luke 22, 27 - 30)

SHEEP

Sheep in the Midst of Wolves

Jesus (to his disciples):

ehold, I send you out as sheep in the midst of wolves; so be wise as serpents and innocent as doves. Beware of men; for they will deliver you up to councils, and flog you in their synagogues, and you will be dragged before governors and kings for my sake, to bear testimony before them and the Gentiles. When they deliver you up, do not be anxious how you are to speak or what you are to say; for what you are to say will be given to you in that hour; for it is not you who speak, but the Spirit of your Father speaking through you.

(Matthew 10, 16 - 20; Luke 10, 3)

SIGNS

These Signs Are Written That You May Believe That Jesus Is the Christ, the Son of God

John the Apostle:

ow Jesus did many other signs in the presence of the disciples, which are not written in this book; but these are written that you may believe that Jesus is the Christ, the Son of God, and that believing you may have life in his name.

(John 20, 30. 31)

The Signs Will Accompany Those Who Believe

Jesus (to the eleven):

o into all the world and preach the gospel to the whole creation. He who believes and is baptized will be saved; but he who does not believe will be condemned. And these signs will accompany those who believe: in my name they will cast out demons; they will speak in new tongues; they will pick up serpents, and if they drink any deadly thing, it will not hurt them; they will lay their hands on the sick, and they will recover.

(Mark 16, 15 - 18; Luke 10, 19)

A SERIES OF JESUS' POWERFUL WORDS

SIN

If You Were Blind, You Would Have No Guilt

Jesus (to a man blind from his birth):

or judgment I came into this world, that those who do not see may see, and that those who see may become blind.

Some of the Pharisees near him heard this, and they said to him:

♦ *Are we also blind?*

Jesus said to them:

♦ *If you were blind, you would have no guilt; but now that you say, 'We see,' your guilt remains.*

(John 9, 39 - 41)

Woe to the Man Who Causes One of These Little Ones Who Believe in Me to Sin

t that time the disciples came to Jesus, saying:

♦ *Who is the greatest in the kingdom of heaven?*

And calling to him a child, he put him in the midst of them, and said:

♦ *Truly, I say to you, unless you turn and become like children, you will never enter the kingdom of heaven.*

Whoever humbles himself like this child, he is the greatest in the kingdom of heaven.

THE TEACHINGS OF JESUS

Whoever receives one such child in my name receives me; but whoever causes one of these little ones who believe in me to sin, it would be better for him to have a great millstone fastened round his neck and to be drowned in the depth of the sea.

(Matthew 18, 1 - 6; Mark 9, 35 - 37; Luke 9, 46 - 48)

They Have Seen and Hated Both Me and My Father

Jesus (to his disciples):

f I had not done among them the works which no one else did, they would not have sin; but now they have seen and hated both me and my Father.

(John 15, 24)

They Have No Excuse for Their Sin

Jesus (to his disciples):

f I had not come and spoken to them, they would not have sin; but now they have no excuse for their sin.

(John 15, 22)

SINNERS

I Came Not to Call the Righteous, but Sinners

Jesus (to the Pharisees):

hose who are well have no need of a physician, but those who are sick. Go and learn what this means, `I desire mercy, and not sacrifice.' For I came not to call the righteous,

A SERIES OF JESUS' POWERFUL WORDS

but sinners.

(Matthew 9, 12. 13)

Be Merciful, Even As Your Father Is Merciful
(The Sermon on the Mount)

Jesus (to his disciples and a great multitude
of people from all Judea and Jerusalem
and the seacost of Tyre and Sidon):

nd as you wish that men would do to you, do so to them. If you love those who love you, what credit is that to you? For even sinners love those who love them. And if you do good to those who do good to you, what credit is that to you?

For even sinners do the same. And if you lend to those from whom you hope to receive, what credit is that to you? Even sinners lend to sinners, to receive as much again.

But love your enemies, and do good, and lend, expecting nothing in return; and your reward will be great, and you will be sons of the Most High; for he is kind to the ungrateful and the selfish. Be merciful, even as your Father is merciful.

(Luke 6, 31 - 36, Matthew 5, 43 – 48)

SLANDER

Out of the Heart of Man, Come Evil Thoughts

nd he (Jesus) called the people to him again, and said to them:

♦ *Hear me, all of you, and understand: there is nothing*

outside a man which by going into him can defile him; but the things which come out of a man are what defile him.

And when he had entered the house, and left the people, his disciples asked him about the parable. And he said to them:

♦ *Then are you also without understanding? Do you not see that whatever goes into a man from outside cannot defile him, since it enters, not his heart but his stomach, and so passes on?*

(Thus he declared all foods clean.)

And he said:

♦ *What comes out of a man is what defiles a man. For from within, out of the heart of man, come evil thoughts, fornication, theft, murder, adultery, coveting, wickedness, deceit, licentiousness, envy, slander, pride, foolishness. All these evil things come from within, and they defile a man.*

(Mark 7, 14 - 23;   Matthew 15, 10 - 20)

SLAVE

Whoever Would Be First Among You Must Be Your Slave

nd when the ten heard it (the mother of the sons of Zebedee asked Jesus: "Command that these two sons of mine may sit, one at your right hand and one at your left, in your kingdom") they were indignant at the two brothers. But Jesus called them to him and said:

♦ *You know that the rulers of the Gentiles lord it over them, and their great men exercise authority over them. It shall not be so among you; but whoever would be great among you must be your* servant, and whoever would be first among you must be your slave; even as the Son of man came not to be served but to serve, and to give his life as a ransom for many.

(Matthew 20, 24 - 28; Mark 9, 35; 10, 41 - 45; Luke 22, 24 - 26)

SON OF MAN

You Will See the Son of Man Seated at the Right Hand of Power, and Coming on the Clouds of Heaven

ut Jesus was silent. And the high priest said to him:

♦ *I adjure you by the living God, tell us if you are the Christ, the Son of God.*

Jesus said to him:

♦ *You have said so. But I tell you, hereafter you will see the Son of man seated at the right hand of Power, and coming on the clouds of heaven.*

(Matthew 26, 63. 64, Luke 22, 67 - 69)

They Will See the Son of Man Coming on the Clouds of Heaven with Power and Great Glory

Jesus (to his disciples):

or as the lightning comes from the east and shines as far as the west, so will be the coming of the Son of man. Wherever the body is, there the eagles will be gathered together.

Immediately after the tribulation of those days the sun will be darkened, and the moon will not give its light, and the stars will fall from heaven, and the powers of the heavens will be shaken; then will appear the sign of the Son of man in heaven, and then all the tribes of the earth will mourn, and they will see the Son of man coming on the clouds of heaven with power and great glory; and he will send out his angels with a loud trumpet call, and they will gather his elect from the four winds, from one end of heaven to the other.

(Matthew 24, 27 - 31; Mark 13, 24 - 27)

SONS OF LIGHT

Believe in the Light, That You May Become Sons of Light

Jesus (to his disciples and the crowds):

he light is with you for a little longer. Wake while you have the light, lest the darkness overtake you; he who wakes in the darkness does not know where he goes. While you have the light, believe in the light, that you may become sons of light.

(John 12, 35. 36)

SPARROWS

You Are of More Value Than Many Sparrows

Jesus (to his disciples):

re not two sparrows sold for a penny? And not one of them will fall to the ground without your Father's will. But even the hairs of your head are all numbered. Fear not, therefore; you are of more value than many sparrows.

(Matthew 10, 29 - 31; Luke 12, 6. 7)

A SERIES OF JESUS' POWERFUL WORDS

SPECK

You Hypocrite, First Take the Log Out of Your Own Eye
(The Sermon on the Mount)

nd great crowds followed him (Jesus) from Galilee and the Decapolis and Jerusalem and Judea and from beyond the Jordan. Seeing the crowds, he went up on the mountain, and when he sat down his disciples came to him. And he opened his mouth and taught them, saying:

♦ *Why do you see the speck that is in your brother's eye, but do not notice the log that is in your own eye? Or how can you say to your brother, 'Let me take the speck out of your eye,' when there is the log in your own eye? You hypocrite, first take the log out of your own eye, and then you will see clearly to take the speck out of your brother's eye.*

(Matthew 4, 25; 5, 1. 2; 7, 3 - 5; Luke 6, 17 - 21; 41. 42)

SPIRIT

Blessed Are the Poor in Spirit
(The Sermon on the Mount)

nd great crowds followed him (Jesus) from Galilee and the Decapolis and Jerusalem and Judea and from beyond the Jordan. Seeing the crowds, he went up on the mountain, and when he sat down his disciples came to him. And he opened his mouth and taught them, saying:

♦ *Blessed are the poor in spirit, for theirs is the kingdom of heaven.*

(Matthew 4, 25; 5, 1 -3; Luke 6, 17 - 20)

The Spirit Indeed Is Willing, but the Flesh Is Weak

nd he (Jesus) came to the disciples and found them sleeping; and he said to Peter:

♦ *So, could you not watch with me one hour? Watch and pray that you may not enter into temptation; the spirit indeed is willing, but the flesh is weak.*

(Matthew 26, 40. 41; Mark 14, 37. 38; Luke 22, 45. 46)

The Spirit Gives Life

Jesus (to his disciples):

*t is the spirit that gives life, the flesh is of no avail; the words that I have spoken to you are spirit and life.*

(John 6, 63)

SPIRIT DUMB AND DEAF

This Kind Cannot Be Driven Out by Anything but Prayer

nd when he (Jesus) had entered the house, his disciples asked him privately:

♦ *Why could we not cast it out?*

And he said to them:

♦ *This kind cannot be driven out by anything but prayer.*

(Mark 9, 28. 29)

A SERIES OF JESUS' POWERFUL WORDS

SPIRIT OF GOD

Jesus Casts Out Demons by the Spirit of God

Jesus (to the Pharisees):

 *ut if it is by the Spirit of God that I cast out demons, then the kingdom of God has come upon you.*

(Matthew 12, 28; Luke 11, 20)

SPIRIT (HOLY SPIRIT)

Unless One Is Born of Water and the Spirit, He Cannot Enter the Kingdom of God

Jesus (to Nicodemus):

 *ruly, truly, I say to you, unless one is born of water and the Spirit, he cannot enter the kingdom of God. That which is born of the flesh is flesh, and that which is born of the Spirit is spirit. Do not marvel that I said to you, `You must be born anew.' The wind blows where it wills, and you hear the sound of it, but you do not know whence it comes or whither it goes; so it is with every one who is born of the Spirit.*

(John 3, 5 - 8)

Whoever Blasphemes Against the Holy Spirit Never Has Forgiveness

Jesus (to his disciples and the crowds):

 *ruly, I say to you, all sins will be forgiven the sons of men, and whatever blasphemies they utter; but whoever blasphemes against the Holy Spirit never has forgiveness, but is guilty*

of an eternal sin.

(Mark 3, 28. 29)

♦ *And whoever says a word against the Son of man will be forgiven; but whoever speaks against the Holy Spirit will not be forgiven, either in this age or in the age to come.*

(Matthew 12, 32)

STEAL

You Shall Not Steal

Jesus (to the rich young man):

If you would enter life, keep the commandments.

He said to him:

♦ *Which?*

And Jesus said:

♦ *You shall not kill, You shall not commit adultery, You shall not steal, You shall not bear false witness, Honor your father and mother, and, You shall love your neighbor as yourself.*

The young man said to him:

♦ *All these I have observed; what do I still lack?*

Jesus said to him:

♦ *If you would be perfect, go, sell what you possess and give to the poor, and you will have treasure in heaven; and come, follow me.*

When the young man heard this he went away sorrowful; for he had great possessions.

(Matthew 19, 17 - 22; Mark 10, 19 - 22; Luke 18, 20 - 23)

A SERIES OF JESUS' POWERFUL WORDS

SWEAR

Do Not Swear at All

(The Sermon on the Mount)

Jesus (to his disciples and the crowds):

gain you have heard that it was said to the men of old, `You shall not swear falsely, but shall perform to the Lord what you have sworn.' But I say to you, Do not swear at all, either by heaven, for it is the throne of God, or by the earth, for it is his footstool, or by Jerusalem, for it is the city of the great King. And do not swear by your head, for you cannot make one hair white or black. Let what you say be simply `Yes' or `No'; anything more than this comes from evil.

(Matthew 5, 33 - 37)

SWORD

All Who Take the Sword Will Perish by the Sword

Jesus (to one of his disciples):

ut your sword back into its place; for all who take the sword will perish by the sword.

(Matthew 26, 52; Mark 14, 47; Luke 22, 50)

I Have Not Come to Bring Peace, but a Sword

Jesus (to his twelve disciples):

o not think that I have come to bring peace on earth; I have not come to bring peace, but a sword. For I have come to set a man against his father, and a daughter against her

mother, and a daughter-in-law against her mother-in-law; and a man's foes will be those of his own household.

(Matthew 10, 34 – 36)

TAX COLLECTOR

If Your Brother Refuses to Listen Let Him Be to You As a Gentile and a Tax Collector

Jesus (to his disciples):

If your brother sins against you, go and tell him his fault, between you and him alone. If he listens to you, you have gained your brother. But if he does not listen, take one or two others along with you, that every word may be confirmed by the evidence of two or three witnesses.

If he refuses to listen to them, tell it to the church; and if he refuses to listen even to the church, let him be to you as a Gentile and a tax collector.

(Matthew 18, 15 - 17)

TEACHER

You Call Me Teacher and Lord

When he (Jesus) had washed their feet, and taken his garments, and resumed his place, he said to them:

♦ *Do you know what I have done to you? You call me Teacher and Lord; and you are right, for so I am. If I then, your Lord and Teacher, have washed your feet, you also ought to wash one another's feet. For I have given you an example, that you also should do as I have done to you.*

A SERIES OF JESUS' POWERFUL WORDS

Truly, truly, I say to you, a servant is not greater than his master; nor is he who is sent greater than he who sent him.

If you know these things, blessed are you if you do them.

(John 13, 12 - 17)

A Disciple Is Not Above His Teacher
(The Sermon on the Mount)

Jesus (to his disciples and a great multitude
of people from all Judea and Jerusalem
and the seacost of Tyre and Sidon):

an a blind man lead a blind man? Will they not both fall into a pit? A disciple is not above his teacher, but every one when he is fully taught will be like his teacher.

A disciple is not above his teacher, but every one when he is fully taught will be like his teacher.

(Luke 6, 39. 40; Matthew 15, 14; 10, 24; John 13, 16)

You Have One Teacher, the Christ

Jesus (to his disciples):

ut you are not to be called rabbi, for you have one teacher, and you are all brethren.

And call no man your father on earth, for you have one Father, who is in heaven.

Neither be called masters, for you have one master, the Christ.

(Matthew 23, 8 - 10)

TEMPTATION

Watch and Pray That You May Not Enter into Temptation

Jesus (to Peter, James and John):

atch and pray that you may not enter into temptation; the spirit indeed is willing, but the flesh is weak.

(Matthew 26, 41; Mark 14, 38; Luke 22, 46)

Woe to the World for Temptations to Sin!

Jesus (to his disciples):

oe to the world for temptations to sin! For it is necessary that temptations come, but woe to the man by whom the temptation comes! And if your hand or your foot causes you to sin, cut it off and throw it away; it is better for you to enter life maimed or lame than with two hands or two feet to be thrown into the eternal fire.

And if your eye causes you to sin, pluck it out and throw it away; it is better for you to enter life with one eye than with two eyes to be thrown into the hell of fire.

(Matthew 18, 7 - 9; 5, 29. 30; Mark 9, 43 - 49; Luke 17, 1)

Woe to the Man Who Causes One of These Little Ones Who Believe in Me to Sin

nd he (Jesus) took a child, and put him in the midst of them; and taking him in his arms, he said to them:

♦ *Whoever receives one such child in my name receives*

A SERIES OF JESUS' POWERFUL WORDS

me; and whoever receives me, receives not me but him who sent me.

Whoever causes one of these little ones who believe in me to sin, it would be better for him if a great millstone were hung round his neck and he were thrown into the sea.

(Mark 9, 36. 37. 42; Matthew 18, 5. 6; Luke 17, 2)

TESTIMONY

We Speak of What We Know, and Bear Witness to What We Have Seen

Jesus (to Nicodemus):

ruly, truly, I say to you, we speak of what we know, and bear witness to what we have seen; but you do not receive our testimony. If I have told you earthly things and you do not believe, how can you believe if I tell you heavenly things?

(John 3, 11. 12)

THEFT

Out of the Heart of Man, Come Evil Thoughts

nd he (Jesus) called the people to him again, and said to them:

♦ *Hear me, all of you, and understand: there is nothing outside a man which by going into him can defile him; but the things which come out of a man are what defile him.*

And when he had entered the house, and left the people, his disciples asked him about the parable. And he said to them:

♦ *Then are you also without understanding? Do you not see that whatever goes into a man from outside cannot defile him, since it enters, not his heart but his stomach, and so passes on?*

(Thus he declared all foods clean.)

And he said:

♦ *What comes out of a man is what defiles a man. For from within, out of the heart of man, come evil thoughts, fornication, theft, murder, adultery, coveting, wickedness, deceit, licentiousness, envy, slander, pride, foolishness. All these evil things come from within, and they defile a man.*

And from there he arose and went away to the region of Tyre and Sidon.

(Mark 7, 14 - 24; Matthew 15, 10 - 21)

THIRST

Blessed Are Those Who Hunger and Thirst for Righteousness

(The Sermon on the Mount)

nd great crowds followed him (Jesus) from Galilee and the Decapolis and Jerusalem and Judea and from beyond the Jordan. Seeing the crowds, he went up on the mountain, and when he sat down his disciples came to him.

And he opened his mouth and taught them, saying:

♦ *Blessed are those who hunger and thirst for righteousness, for they shall be satisfied.*

(Matthew 4, 25; 5, 1. 2. 6; Luke 6, 17 - 21)

A SERIES OF JESUS' POWERFUL WORDS

TOMBS

All Who Are in the Tombs Will Hear His Voice

Jesus (to the Jews):

ruly, truly, I say to you, the hour is coming, and now is, when the dead will hear the voice of the Son of God, and those who hear will live. For as the Father has life in himself, so he has granted the Son also to have life in himself, and has given him authority to execute judgment, because he is the Son of man.

Do not marvel at this; for the hour is coming when all who are in the tombs will hear his voice and come forth, those who have done good, to the resurrection of life, and those who have done evil, to the resurrection of judgment.

(John 5, 25 - 29)

TRADITION

This People Honors Me with Their Lips, but Their Heart is Far from Me

Jesus (to the Pharisees and the scribes):

ell did Isaiah prophesy of you hypocrites, as it is written, `This people honors me with their lips, but their heart is far from me; in vain do they worship me, teaching as doctrines the precepts of men.'

You leave the commandment of God, and hold fast the tradition of men.

And he said to them:

THE TEACHINGS OF JESUS

♦ *You have a fine way of rejecting the commandment of God, in order to keep your tradition!*

(Mark 7, 6 - 9; Matthew 15, 7 - 9)

TREASURE

Where Your Treasure Is, There Will Your Heart Be Also
(The Sermon on the Mount)

nd great crowds followed him (Jesus) from Galilee and the Decapolis and Jerusalem and Judea and from beyond the Jordan. Seeing the crowds, he went up on the mountain, and when he sat down his disciples came to him. And he opened his mouth and taught them, saying:

♦ *Do not lay up for yourselves treasures on earth, where moth and rust consume and where thieves break in and steal, but lay up for yourselves treasures in heaven, where neither moth nor rust consumes and where thieves do not break in and steal. For where your treasure is, there will your heart be also.*

(Matthew 6, 19 - 21; Luke 12, 21. 33. 34)

TRESPASSES

Forgive, That Your Father Also Who Is in Heaven May Forgive You Your Trespasses

Jesus (to his disciples):

nd whenever you stand praying, forgive, if you have anything against any one; so that your Father also who is in heaven may forgive you your trespasses.

(Mark 11, 25)

215

A SERIES OF JESUS' POWERFUL WORDS

If You Do Not Forgive Men Their Trespasses, Neither Will Your Father Forgive Your Trespasses

(The Sermon on the Mount)

Jesus (to his disciples and the crowds):

or if you forgive men their trespasses, your heavenly Father also will forgive you; but if you do not forgive men their trespasses, neither will your Father forgive your trespasses.

(Matthew 6, 14. 15; Mark 11, 25. 26; Luke 6, 37)

TRIBULATION

In the World You Have Tribulation

Jesus (to his disciples):

n the world you have tribulation; but be of good cheer, I have overcome the world.

(John 16, 33)

TROUBLE

Let the Day's Own Trouble Be Sufficient for the Day

(The Sermon on the Mount)

Jesus (to his disciples and the crowds):

herefore I tell you, do not be anxious about your life, what you shall eat or what you shall drink, nor about your body, what you shall put on. Is not life more than food, and the body more than clothing?

Look at the birds of the air: they neither sow nor reap nor gather into barns, and yet your heavenly Father feeds them. Are you not of more value than they?

And which of you by being anxious can add one cubit to his span of life? And why are you anxious about clothing? Consider the lilies of the field, how they grow; they neither toil nor spin; yet I tell you, even Solomon in all his glory was not arrayed like one of these. But if God so clothes the grass of the field, which today is alive and tomorrow is thrown into the oven, will he not much more clothe you, O men of little faith?

Therefore do not be anxious, saying, `What shall we eat?' or `What shall we drink?' or `What shall we wear?' For the Gentiles seek all these things; and your heavenly Father knows that you need them all. But seek first his kingdom and his righteousness, and all these things shall be yours as well.

Therefore do not be anxious about tomorrow, for tomorrow will be anxious for itself. Let the day's own trouble be sufficient for the day.

(Matthew 6, 25 – 34; Luke 12, 22 – 31)

TRUTH

If You Continue in My Word, You Will Know the Truth

esus then said to the Jews who had believed in him:

♦ *If you continue in my word, you are truly my disciples and you will know the truth, and the truth will make you free.*

They answered him:

♦ *We are descendants of Abraham, and have never been in bondage to any one. How is it that you say, `You will be made free'?*

Jesus answered them:

♦ *Truly, truly, I say to you, every one who commits sin is a slave to sin. The slave does not continue in the house for ever; the son continues for ever. So if the Son makes you free, you will be free indeed. I know that you are descendants of Abraham; yet you seek to kill me, because my word finds no place in you.*

(John 8, 31 - 37)

UNCHASTITY

Whoever Divorces His Wife, Except for Unchastity, and Marries Another, Commits Adultery

ow when Jesus had finished these sayings, he went away from Galilee and entered the region of Judea beyond the Jordan; and large crowds followed him, and he healed them there. And Pharisees came up to him and tested him by asking:

♦ *Is it lawful to divorce one's wife for any cause?*

He answered:

♦ *Have you not read that he who made them from the beginning made them male and female, and said, `For this reason a man shall leave his father and mother and be joined to his wife, and the two shall become one flesh'? So they are no longer two but one flesh. What therefore God has joined together, let not man put asunder.*

They said to him:

♦ *Why then did Moses command one to give a certificate of divorce, and to put her away?*

He said to them:

♦ *For your hardness of heart Moses allowed you to divorce your wives, but from the beginning it was not so. And I say to you: whoever divorces his wife, except for unchastity, and marries another, commits adultery.*

The disciples said to him:

♦ *If such is the case of a man with his wife, it is not expedient to marry.*

But he said to them:

♦ *Not all men can receive this saying, but only those to whom it is given. For there are eunuchs who have been so from birth, and there are eunuchs who have been made eunuchs by men, and there are eunuchs who have made themselves eunuchs for the sake of the kingdom of heaven.*

He who is able to receive this, let him receive it.

(Matthew 19, 1 - 12; 5, 31. 32; Mark 10, 1 - 12; Luke 16, 18)

VICTOR

I Have Overcome the World

Jesus (to his disciples):

n the world you have tribulation; but be of good cheer, I have overcome the world.

(John 16, 33)

A SERIES OF JESUS' POWERFUL WORDS

VINE

The Branch Cannot Bear Fruit by Itself, Unless It Abides in the Vine

Jesus (to his disciples):

bide in me, and I in you. As the branch cannot bear fruit by itself, unless it abides in the vine, neither can you, unless you abide in me.

(John 15, 4)

Apart from Me You Can Do Nothing

Jesus (to his disciples):

bide in me, and I in you. As the branch cannot bear fruit by itself, unless it abides in the vine, neither can you, unless you abide in me. I am the vine, you are the branches. He who abides in me, and I in him, he it is that bears much fruit, for apart from me you can do nothing. If a man does not abide in me, he is cast forth as a branch and withers; and the branches are gathered, thrown into the fire and burned.

(John 15, 4 - 6)

WATCH AT ALL TIMES

Watch at All Times, Praying to Escape All That Will Take Place

Jesus (to his disciples):

ut take heed to yourselves lest your hearts be weighed down with dissipation and drunkenness and cares of this life, and that day come upon you suddenly like a snare; for it will come upon all who dwell upon the face of the whole earth.

THE TEACHINGS OF JESUS

But watch at all times, praying that you may have strength to escape all these things that will take place, and to stand before the Son of man.

(Luke 21, 34 - 36;   Matthew 24, 42;   25, 13;   Mark   13, 33)

The Son of Man Is Coming at an Hour You Do Not Expect

Jesus (to his disciples):

atch therefore, for you do not know on what day your Lord is coming.

(Matthew 24, 42;   Mark 13, 33. 35;   Luke 21, 36)

Watch and Pray

Jesus (to Peter, James and John):

atch and pray that you may not enter into temptation; the spirit indeed is willing, but the flesh is weak.

(Matthew 26, 41;   Mark 14, 38;   Luke 22, 46)

You Also Must Be Ready for the Son of Man Is Coming at an Unexpected Hour

Jesus (to his disciples and the crowds):

et your loins be girded and your lamps burning, and be like men who are waiting for their master to come home from the marriage feast, so that they may open to him at once when he comes and knocks.

Blessed are those servants whom the master finds awake when he comes; truly, I say to you, he will gird himself and have them sit at table, and he will come and serve them.

If he comes in the second watch, or in the third, and finds them so, blessed are those servants!

But know this, that if the householder had known at what hour the thief was coming, he would not have left his house to be broken into.

You also must be ready; for the Son of man is coming at an unexpected hour.

(Luke 12, 35 - 40;   Matthew 24, 43. 44)

WICKEDNESS

Out of the Heart of Man, Come Evil Thoughts

And he (Jesus) called the people to him again, and said to them:

♦ *Hear me, all of you, and understand: there is nothing outside a man which by going into him can defile him; but the things which come out of a man are what defile him.*

And when he had entered the house, and left the people, his disciples asked him about the parable. And he said to them:

♦ *Then are you also without understanding? Do you not see that whatever goes into a man from outside cannot defile him, since it enters, not his heart but his stomach, and so passes on?*

(Thus he declared all foods clean.)

And he said:

♦ *What comes out of a man is what defiles a man. For from within, out of the heart of man, come evil thoughts, fornication, theft, murder, adultery, coveting, wickedness, deceit, licentiousness, envy, slander, pride, foolishness. All these evil things come from within, and they defile a man.*

(Mark 7, 14 - 23;   Matthew 15, 10 - 20)

WITNESS

You Shall Not Bear False Witness

Jesus (to the rich young man):

f you would enter life, keep the commandments.

He said to him:

♦ *Which?*

And Jesus said:

♦ *You shall not kill, You shall not commit adultery, You shall not steal, You shall not bear false witness, Honor your father and mother, and, You shall love your neighbor as yourself.*

The young man said to him:

♦ *All these I have observed; what do I still lack?*

Jesus said to him:

♦ *If you would be perfect, go, sell what you possess and give to the poor, and you will have treasure in heaven; and come, follow me.*

When the young man heard this he went away sorrowful; for he had great possessions.

(Matthew 19, 17 - 22;   Mark 10, 19 - 22;   Luke 18, 20 - 23)

A SERIES OF JESUS' POWERFUL WORDS

WOLVES

Sheep in the Midst of Wolves

Jesus (to his disciples):

ehold, I send you out as sheep in the midst of wolves; so be wise as serpents and innocent as doves. Beware of men; for they will deliver you up to councils, and flog you in their synagogues, and you will be dragged before governors and kings for my sake, to bear testimony before them and the Gentiles. When they deliver you up, do not be anxious how you are to speak or what you are to say; for what you are to say will be given to you in that hour; for it is not you who speak, but the Spirit of your Father speaking through you.

(Matthew 10, 16 - 20; Luke 10, 3)

WORD OF GOD

The Seed Is the Word of God

nd when his disciples asked him (Jesus) what this parable meant, he said:

♦ *To you it has been given to know the secrets of the kingdom of God; but for others they are in parables, so that seeing they may not see, and hearing they may not understand.*

Now the parable is this: The seed is the word of God. The ones along the path are those who have heard; then the devil comes and takes away the word from their hearts, that they may not believe and be saved. And the ones on the rock are those who, when they hear the word, receive it with joy; but these have no root, they believe for a while and in time of temptation fall away. And as

THE TEACHINGS OF JESUS

for what fell among the thorns, they are those who hear, but as they go on their way they are choked by the cares and riches and pleasures of life, and their fruit does not mature. And as for that in the good soil, they are those who, hearing the word, hold it fast in an honest and good heart, and bring forth fruit with patience.

(Luke 8, 9 – 15)

Man shall not live by bread alone, but by every word that proceeds from the mouth of God

nd the tempter came and said to him (to Jesus):

◆ *If you are the Son of God, command these stones to become loaves of bread.*

But he answered:

◆ *It is written, `Man shall not live by bread alone, but by every word that proceeds from the mouth of God.*

(Matthew 4, 3. 4)

WORD OF JESUS

If any One Keeps My Word, He Will Never See Death

Jesus (to the Jews):

*ruly, truly, I say to you, if any one keeps my word, he will never see death.*

(John 8, 51)

A SERIES OF JESUS' POWERFUL WORDS

He Who Hears My Word and Believes Him Who Sent Me, Has Eternal Life

Jesus (to the Jews):

ruly, truly, I say to you, he who hears my word and believes him who sent me, has eternal life; he does not come into judgment, but has passed from death to life.

(John 5, 24)

If You Continue in My Word, You Will Know the Truth

esus then said to the Jews who had believed in him:

♦ *If you continue in my word, you are truly my disciples and you will know the truth, and the truth will make you free.*

(John 8, 31. 32)

WORLD

What Will It Profit a Man, if He Gains the Whole World and Forfeits His Life?

Jesus (to his disciples):

f any man would come after me, let him deny himself and take up his cross and follow me. For whoever would save his life will lose it, and whoever loses his life for my sake will find it. For what will it profit a man, if he gains the whole world and forfeits his life?

Or what shall a man give in return for his life?

THE TEACHINGS OF JESUS

For the Son of man is to come with his angels in the glory of his Father, and then he will repay every man for what he has done.

(Matthew 16, 24 - 27; Mark 8, 36. 37; Luke 9, 25)

You shall worship the Lord your God and Him Only Shall You Serve

gain, the devil took him (Jesus) to a very high mountain, and showed him all the kingdoms of the world and the glory of them; and he said to him:

♦ *All these I will give you, if you will fall down and worship me.*

Then Jesus said to him:

♦ *Begone, Satan! for it is written, `You shall worship the Lord your God and him only shall you serve.'*

(Matthew 4, 8 – 10)

Because You Are Not of the World, Therefore the World Hates You

Jesus (to his disciples):

*f the world hates you, know that it has hated me before it hated you. If you were of the world, the world would love its own; but because you are not of the world, but I chose you out of the world, therefore the world hates you. Remember the word that I said to you, `A servant is not greater than his master.' If they persecuted me, they will persecute you; if they kept my word, they will keep yours also. But all this they will do to you on my account, because they do not know him who sent me.*

(John 15, 18 - 21)

I Have Overcome the World

Jesus (to his disciples):

n the world you have tribulation; but be of good cheer, I have overcome the world.

(John 16, 33)

YOKE

My Yoke Is Easy, and My Burden Is Light

Jesus (to his disciples and the crowds):

ome to me, all who labor and are heavy laden, and I will give you rest. Take my yoke upon you, and learn from me; for I am gentle and lowly in heart, and you will find rest for your souls. For my yoke is easy, and my burden is light.

(Matthew 11, 28 - 30)

CONTENTS

ABIDE 1
    Abide in Me 1
    If You Abide in Me Ask Whatever You Will 1

ABOMINATION 1
    What Is Exalted Among Men Is an Abomination in the Sight of God 1

ADULTERY 2
    You Shall Not Commit Adultery 2
    Whoever Divorces His Wife, Except for Unchastity, Commits Adultery 2
    Every One Who Looks at a Woman Lustfully Has Already Committed Adultery 4
    Out of the Heart of Man, Come Evil Thoughts 4

AGE 5
    I Am with You Always, to the Close of the Age 5

ANGRY 5
    Every One Who Is Angry with His Brother Shall Be Liable to Judgment 5

A SERIES OF JESUS' POWERFUL WORDS

ANXIOUS   6

    Do Not Be Anxious About Your Life   6

ASK   7

    Every One Who Asks Receives, and He Who Seeks Finds, and to Him Who Knocks It Will Be Opened   7
    If You Ask Anything of the Father, He Will Give It to You in My Name   7
    Whatever You Ask in My Name, I Will Do It   8
    If You Abide in Me Ask Whatever You Will   8

AUTHORITY   8

    All Authority in Heaven and on Earth Has Been Given to Me   8
    Power and Authority overall All Demons   9
    For with Authority and Power Jesus Commands the Unclean Spirits?   9

BAPTIZE   10

    He Who Believes and Is Baptized Will Be Saved   10
    Make Disciples of All Nations, Baptizing Them in the Name of the Father and of the Son and of the Holy Spirit   10

BEAR FALSE WITNESS   11

    You Shall Not Bear False Witness   11

BEATING   12

    A Servant Who Did Not Act According to Master's Will Would Receive a Severe Beating   12

BELIEVE 12

>Whoever Lives and Believes in Me Shall Never Die   12
>All Things Are Possible to Him Who Believes   12
>These Signs Are Written That You May Believe That Jesus Is the Christ, the Son of God   13
>If My Words Abide in You, Ask Whatever You Will   13
>He Who Hears My Word and Believes Him Who Sent Me, Has Eternal Life   14
>Blessed Are Those Who Have Not Seen and yet Believe   14
>He Who Believes and Is Baptized Will Be Saved   14
>I Have Told You Earthly Things and You Do Not Believe   15

BIRDS 15

>Birds Neither Sow Nor Reap Nor Gather into Barns, and yet Your Heavenly Father Feeds Them   15

BIRTH 16

>Unless One Is Born of Water and the Spirit, He Cannot Enter the Kingdom of God   16

BLASPHEME 17

>Whoever Blasphemes Against the Holy Spirit Never Has Forgiveness   17
>Whoever Speaks Against the Holy Spirit Will Not Be Forgiven   17

BLESSED 17

>The Beatitudes   17
>Blessed Are Those Who Have Not Seen and Yet Belie-

ve 18

You Will Be Blessed, Because They Cannot Repay
You 18

BLIND 19

When You Give a Feast, Invite the Poor, the Maimed,
the Lame, and the Blind 19

BLOOD 19

He Who Eats My Flesh and Drinks My Blood I Will
Raise Him Up at the Last Day 19

BOAST 20

I Will All the More Gladly Boast of My Weaknesses
20

BODY 20

Is Not Life More Than Food, and the Body More Than
Clothing? 20

BORROW 22

Do Not Refuse Him Who Would Borrow from You 22

BRANCH 22

As the Branch Cannot Bear Fruit by Itself, Apart from
Me You Can Do Nothing 22

BROTHER SINS 23

If Your Brother Sins Against You, Go and Tell Him 23

BURDEN   23

My Yoke Is Easy, and My Burden Is Light   23

CALLED   24

Many Are Called   24

CARES OF THIS LIFE   24

Take Heed to Yourselves Lest Your Hearts Be Weighed Down with Cares of This Life   24
Do Not Be Anxious About Tomorrow   24

CARELESS WORD   25

On The Day of Judgment Men Will Render Account for Every Careless Word They Utter   25

CHILD   26

Humble Himself Like a Child   26
Their Angels Always Behold the Face of My Father   26
Receive the Kingdom of God Like a Child   27

CHOSEN   27

Few Are Chosen   27

CHRIST   27

Whose Son Is the Christ?   27
If any Man Would Come After Me, Let Him Deny Himself and Take Up His Cross and Follow Me   28
You Are the Christ, the Son of the Living God   28

CLOTHING 29

    Is Not Life More Than Food, and The Body More Than Clothing? 29

CLOUDS OF HEAVEN 30

    You Will See the Son of Man Seated at the Right Hand of Power, and Coming on the Clouds of Heaven 30

COMMANDMENTS 31

    About Commandments 31
    Which Commandment Is the First of All? 31
    If You Would Enter Life, Keep the Commandments 32
    If You Keep My Commandments, You Will Abide in My Love 33
    A New Commandment I Give to You, That You Love One Another 33
    You Are My Friends if You Do What I Command You 34
    He Who Has My Commandments and Keeps Them, Is He Who Loves Me 34

COMMUNION 34

    This Is My Blood of the Covenant, Which Is Poured Out for Many for the Forgiveness of Sins 34

CONDEMNED 35

    He Who Does Not Believe Will Be Condemned 35
    By Your Words You Will Be Condemned 35

COVERED UP 36

    Nothing Is Covered Up That Will Not Be Revealed 36

COVETOUSNESS — 36

    Out of the Heart of Man, Come Evil Thoughts 36
    Beware of All Covetousness 37

CRITICISM — 37

    Judge Not, That You Be Not Judged 37
    The Measure You Give Will Be the Measure You Get 38

DARKNESS — 38

    Who Walks in the Darkness Does Not Know Where He Goes 38
    When Your Eye Is Not Sound, Your Body Is Full of Darkness 38

DEATH — 39

    Whoever Lives and Believes in Me Shall Never Die 39
    He Who Hears My Word and Believes Him Who Sent Me, Has Passed from Death to Life 39
    There Are Some Standing Here Who Will Not Taste Death 40

DECEIT — 40

    Out of the Heart of Man, Come Evil Thoughts 40

DEMONS — 41

    Jesus Casts Out Demons by the Spirit of God 41
    With Faith the Size of a Mustard Seed 41
    Jesus Casts Out Demons by the Spirit of God 42
    This Kind Cannot Be Driven Out by Anything but Prayer 42

In My Name They Will Cast Out Demons 42

DENY 43

If Any Man Would Come After Me, Let Him Deny Himself and Take Up His Cross and Follow Me 43

DEVIL 43

The Devil Is a Liar and the Father of Lies 43

DISHONEST 44

He Who Is Dishonest in a Very Little Is Dishonest Also in Much 44

DISSIPATION 44

Take Heed to Yourselves Lest Your Hearts Be Weighed Down with Dissipation 44

DIVORCE 44

What Therefore God Has Joined Together, Let Not Man Put Asunder 44

DOOR (GATE) 46

Enter by the Narrow Gate 46
Strive to Enter by the Narrow Door 46

DOVES 47

Be Wise As Serpents and Innocent As Doves 47

DRAW 48

No One Can Come to Me Unless the Father Draws Him 48

DRUNKENNESS   48

    Take Heed to Yourselves, Lest Your Hearts Be Weighed Down with Drunkenness   48

ELECT   49

    His Angels Will Gather His Elect from the Four Winds, from One End of Heaven to the Other   49

ENDURANCE   49

    Gaining Your Lives   49

ENEMIES   50

    Love Your Enemies   50
    Love Your Enemies, Do Good, and Lend, Expecting Nothing in Return   50

ETERNAL LIFE   51

    He Who Eats My Flesh and Drinks My Blood Has Eternal Life   51
    He Who Hears My Word and Believes Him Who Sent Me, Has Eternal Life   51
    He Who Hates His Life in This World Will Keep It for Eternal Life   52
    How to Inherit Eternal Life   52
    If You Would Enter Life, Keep the Commandments   52
    This Is Eternal Life, That They Know Thee, the Only True God and Jesus Christ Whom Thou Hast Sent   53
    I Know That His Commandment Is Eternal Life   53
    Whoever Believes in Jesus Should Not Perish but Have Eternal Life   54
    He Who Believes in the Son Has Eternal Life   54

A SERIES OF JESUS' POWERFUL WORDS

    If Any One Keeps My Word, He Will Never See Death 54
    Come to Me That You May Have Life 55
    Whoever Lives and Believes in Me Shall Never Die 55
    He Who Believes Has Eternal Life 55
    He Who Have Followed Me Will Receive a Hundred fold, and Inherit Eternal Life 55
    He Who Eats This Bread Will Live for Ever 56
    You May Believe That Jesus Is the Christ, the Son of God, and That Believing You May Have Life in His Name 56
    I Know Them, and They Follow Me and I Give Them Eternal Life 57

ENVY   57

    Out of the Heart of Man Come Evil Thoughts 57

EUCHARIST   58

    This Is My Blood of the Covenant, Which Is Poured Out for Many for the Forgiveness of Sins 58

EVIL   58

    Do Not Resist One Who Is Evil 58

EVIL THINGS   59

    The Things Which Come Out of a Man Are What Defile Him 59
    All Who Take the Sword Will Perish by the Sword 60

EVIL THOUGHTS   40

    Out of the Heart of Man, Come Evil Thoughts 40

EXALTED 60

> What Is Exalted Among Men Is an Abomination in the Sight of God   60
> Every One Who Exalts Himself Will Be Humbled   60
> Whoever Exalts Himself Will Be Humbled   61

EYE 61

> Your Eye Is the Lamp of Your Body   61

FAITH 62

> A Faith As a Grain of Mustard Seed   62
> A Little Faith As a Grain of Mustard Seed   62
> Blessed Are Those Who Have Not Seen and yet Believe   63
> If My Words Abide in You, Ask Whatever You Will   63

FAITHFUL 63

> He Who Is Faithful in a Very Little Is Faithful Also in Much   63
> Woe to You, When All Men Speak Well of You   64

FALSE PROPHETS 64

> Woe to You, When All Men Speak Well of You   64
> Beware of False Prophets   64
> Take Heed That No One Leads You Astray   65

FALSE WITNESS 65

> You Shall Not Bear False Witness   65

FAST 66

> The Wedding Guests Do Not Fast While the Bridegroom

Is with Them 66
　　When You Fast, Do Not Look Dismal, Like the Hypo-
　　　crites 67

FATHER AND MOTHER   67

　　Honor Your Father and Mother 67
　　Whoever of You Does Not Renounce All That He Has
　　　Cannot Be My Disciple 68
　　He Who Loves Father or Mother More Than Me Is Not
　　　Worthy of Me 69
　　Honor Your Father and Your Mother 69
　　Every One Who Has Left All, for My Name's Sake, Will
　　　Receive a Hundredfold, and Inherit Eternal Life 69

FATHER'S WILL   70

　　Not One of the Sparrows Will Fall to the Ground Without
　　　Your Father's Will 70

FEAR   70

　　You Are of More Value Than Many Sparrows 70
　　Fear Him Who, After He Has Killed, Has Power to Cast
　　　into Hell 71

FIG   71

　　From the Fig Tree Learn Its Lesson 71

FIRST   72

　　If Any One Would Be First 72
　　He Who Is Greatest Among You 72
　　Some Are First Who Will Be Last 72

FLESH — 73

The Spirit Indeed Is Willing, but the Flesh Is Weak 73
He Who Eats My Flesh and Drinks My Blood I Will
Raise Him Up at the Last Day 73

FOOD — 74

Is Not Life More Than Food, and the Body More Than
Clothing? 74

FOOLISHNESS — 75

Out of the Heart of Man, Come Evil Thoughts 75

FORGIVE — 76

If You Do Not Forgive Men Their Trespasses, Neither
Will Your Father Forgive Your Trespasses 76
Forgive, if You Have Anything Against Any One 76
If Your Brother Sins, Rebuke Him, and if He Repents,
Forgive Him 76
How Often Shall My Brother Sin Against Me 77

FORNICATION — 77

Out of the Heart of Man, Come Evil Thoughts 77

FULL — 78

Woe to You That Are Full Now 78

GATE (DOOR) — 78

Strive to Enter by the Narrow Door 78
Enter by the Narrow Gate 79

GENTILES 80

    If Your Brother Refuses to Listen Let Him Be To You As a Gentile and a Tax Collector 80
    The Gentiles Are Anxious, Saying `What Shall We Eat?' or `What Shall We Drink?' or `What Shall We Wear? 80

GENTLE 81

    I Am Gentle and Lowly in Heart 81

GIVE 82

    Give, and It Will Be Given to You 82
    To Him Who Has Will More Be Given 82
    For to Him Who Has Will More Be Given 82
    Give to Every One Who Begs from You 83
    It Is More Blessed to Give 83

GLORY 83

    They Will See the Son of Man Coming on the Clouds of Heaven with Power and Great Glory 83

GOD 84

    You Cannot Serve God and Mammon 84

GOD'S WILL 84

    Not One of Them Will Fall to the Ground Without Your Father's Will 84

GREATEST 85

    The Greatest in the Kingdom of Heaven? 85
    Who Is Greatest Among You Shall Be Your Servant 85

GUILT   86

    If You Were Blind, You Would Have No Guilt   86

HARVEST   86

    I Sent You to Reap   86
    Pray to the Lord of the Harvest to Send Out Laborers into His Harvest   87

HATE   87

    You Have Heard `Hate Your Enemy` but I Say to You `Love Your Enemies`   87
    They Have Seen and Hated both Me and My Father   88
    You Will Be Hated by All for My Name's Sake   88
    Every One Who Does Evil Hates the Light   88
    The World Hates Me Because I Testify of It That Its Works Are Evil   89
    Because You Are Not of the World, Therefore the World Hates You   89

HEAD OF THE CORNER   90

    The Very Stone Which the Builders Rejected Has Become the Head of the Corner   90

HEARS   90

    The Hairs of Your Head Are All Numbered   90

HEART OF MAN   90

    Blessed Are the Pure in Heart   90
    I Am Gentle and Lowly in Heart   91
    Where Your Treasure Is, There Will Your Heart Be Also   91
    Out of the Abundance of the Heart His Mouth Speaks   92

Out of the Heart of Man, Come Evil Things 92
Take Heed to Yourselves Lest Your Hearts Be Weighed Down with Dissipation and Drunkenness and Cares of This Life 93
This People Honors Me with Their Lips, but Their Heart Is Far from Me 93
God Knows Your Hearts 94
You Shall Love the Lord Your God with All Your Heart 94

HIDDEN   94

Nothing Is Hidden That Will Not Be Known 94

HOLY   95

Do Not Throw Your Pearls Before Swine 95

HOLY COVENANT   95

This Is My Blood of the Covenant, Which Is Poured Out for Many for the Forgiveness of Sins 95

HOLY SPIRIT   96, 206

Whoever Blasphemes Against the Holy Spirit Never Has Forgiveness 96
Whoever Speaks Against the Holy Spirit Will Not Be Forgiven 96

HONOR   97

Honor Your Father and Mother 97
Honor Your Father and Your Mother 98

HUMBLE   98

Whoever Humbles Himself Will Be Exalted 98

He Who Humbles Himself Will Be Exalted   98
We Are Unworthy Servants   99
I Am Among You As One Who Serves   99
To Be Humble Like a Child   100
If Any One Would Be First, He Must Be Last of All   100
Whoever Would Be First Among You Must Be Your Slave   101

HUNGER 101

Blessed Are Those Who Hunger and Thirst for Righteousness   101

HYPOCRITE 102

Beware of the Leaven of the Pharisees, Which Is Hypocrisy   102
Does Not Each of You on the Sabbath Untie His Ox or His Ass from the Manger   102
You Hypocrite, First Take the Log Out of Your Own Eye   103

JERUSALEM 103

Jerusalem Will Be Trodden Down by the Gentiles   103
There Shall Not Be Left Here One Stone Upon Another   104
You Did Not Know the Time of Your Visitation   104
O Jerusalem, Jerusalem, Killing the Prophets   105

JESUS CHRIST, THE SON OF GOD 105

These Signs Are Written That You May Believe That Jesus Is the Christ, the Son Of God   105

JUDGMENT 105

    I Did Not Come to Judge the World but to Save the World 105
    Judge Not, That You Be Not Judged 106
    He Who Hears My Word and Believes Him Who Sent Me, Does Not Come into Judgment 106
    For Judgment I Came into This World 106
    Now Is the Judgment of This World, Now Shall the Ruler of This World Be Cast Out 107
    Woe to You Chorazin and Bethsaida on the Day of Judgment 107
    Whoever Kills Shall Be Liable to Judgment 108

JUSTIFIED 108

    By Your Words You Will Be Justified 108

KILL 109

    You Shall Not Kill 109

KINGDOM OF GOD 110

    I Assign to You a Kingdom 110
    Seek First the Kingdom of God and His Righteousness 110
    No One Who Puts His Hand to the Plow and Looks Back Is Fit for the Kingdom of God 111
    It Is Easier for a Camel to Go Through the Eye of a Needle Than for a Rich Man to Enter the Kingdom of God 112
    The Kingdom of God Will Be Taken Away from You and Given to a Nation Producing the Fruits of It 113
    The Kingdom of God Is Not Coming with Signs to Be

    Observed   113
The Kingdom of God Has Come Upon You   113
The Kingdom of Heaven Has Suffered Violence   114
Not Every One Who Says to Me, `Lord, Lord,' Shall
    Enter the Kingdom of Heaven   115
Seek First Kingdom and His Righteousness   115
Who Is the Greatest in the Kingdom of Heaven?   116
It Will Be Hard for a Rich Man to Enter the Kingdom
    of Heaven   117
It Is Your Father's Good Pleasure to Give You the Kingdom   117
Whoever Does Not Receive the Kingdom of God Like
    a Child Shall Not Enter It   117
Many Will Come from East and West   118
How to Enter the Kingdom of Heaven?   119

KNOCK   119

Every One Who Asks Receives, and He Who Seeks Finds,
    and to Him Who Knocks It Will Be Opened   119

LABOR   120

All Who Labor and Are Heavy Laden, I Will Give You

Rest   120

LADEN   120

All Who Labor and Are Heavy Laden, I Will Give You
    Rest   120

LAME   120

When You Give a Feast, Invite the Poor, the Maimed,
    the Lame, the Blind   120

A SERIES OF JESUS' POWERFUL WORDS

LAMP   121

    Let Your Light So Shine Before Men, That They May See Your Good Works and Give Glory to Your Father Who Is in Heaven   121

    Your Eye Is the Lamp of Your Body   121

LAST   122

    If Any One Would Be First Must Be Last of All   122

    Some Are Last Who Will Be First   122

LAST DAY   123

    He Who Eats My Flesh and Drinks My Blood I Will Raise Him Up at the Last Day   123

    The Word That I Have Spoken Will Be His Judge on the Last Day   123

    That Day Will Come Upon You Suddenly Like a Snare   124

LAW   124

    Not an Iota, Not a Dot, Will Pass from the Law Until All Is Accomplished   124

    All the Prophets and the Law Prophesied Until John   125

    Whatever You Wish That Men Would Do to You, Do So to Them   125

    On the First and Second Commandment Depend All the Law and the Prophets   125

    Do Not Do Good Only to Those Who Do Good to You   126

LEAVEN   126

    Take Heed and Beware of the Leaven of the Pharisees

and Sadducees   126
Beware of the Leaven of the Pharisees, Which Is Hypocrisy   127

LEND   128

Sinners Lend to Sinners, to Receive As Much Again   128

LICENTIOUSNESS   128

Out of the Heart of Man, Come Evil Thoughts   128

LIFE   129

I Am the Resurrection and the Life   129
Is Not Life More Than Food?   129
It Will Be Hard for a Rich Man to Enter the Kingdom of Heaven   130
He Who Hears My Word and Believes Him Who Sent Me, Has Passed from Death to Life   131
How to Gain Your Lives?   131
Whoever Would Save His Life Will Lose It   131
He Who Loves His Life Loses It   132
What Shall a Man Give in Return for His Life?   132

LIGHT   132

Be Careful Lest the Light in You Be Darkness   132
I Have Come As Light into the World   133
Let Your Light Shine Before Men   133
If Any One Walks in the Day, He Does Not Stumble   133
Every One Who Does Evil Hates the Light   134
I Am the Light of the World   134
You Are the Light of the World   134

A SERIES OF JESUS' POWERFUL WORDS

Believe in the Light, That You May Become Sons of Light   135

LOG — 135

You Hypocrite, First Take the Log Out of Your Own Eye   135

LORD — 136

You Call Me Teacher and Lord   136

LORD'S SUPPER — 136

This Is My Blood of the Covenant, Which Is Poured Out for Many for the Forgiveness of Sins   136

LOVE — 137

Greater Love Has No Man   137
Love Your Enemies   137
He Who Loves Me Will Be Loved by My Father   138
He Who Loves Father or Mother More Than Me Is Not Worthy of Me   138
The First and the Second Commandment   138

A New Commandment I Give to You, That You Love One Another   139

LUSTFULLY — 139

Every One Who Looks at a Woman Lustfully Has Already Committed Adultery   139

MAIMED — 140

When You Give a Feast, Invite the Poor, the Maimed,

the Lame, the Blind   140

MAMMON   140
You Cannot Serve God and Mammon   140

MARRIAGE   141
The Two Shall Become One Flesh   141

MASTER   142
No One Can Serve Two Masters   142
A Servant Is Not Greater Than His Master   142

MEASURE   143
To Him Who Has, More Will Be Given   143
The Measure You Give Will Be the Measure You Get   143

MEEK   144
Blessed Are the Meek   144

MERCIFUL   144
Be Merciful, Even As Your Father Is Merciful   144

I Desire Mercy, and Not Sacrifice   145
Go and Learn What This Means, `I Desire Mercy, and Not Sacrifice`   145
Blessed Are the Merciful   145

MOTHER AND FATHER   146
Honor Your Father and Mother   146
He Who Loves Father or Mother More Than Me Is Not Worthy of Me   147

Whoever of You Does Not Renounce All That He Has
    Cannot Be My Disciple 147
Honor Your Father and Your Mother 147
Every One Who Has Left All, for My Name's Sake, Will
    Receive a Hundredfold, and Inherit Eternal Life
    148

MOURN   148

Blessed Are Those Who Mourn 148

MURDER   149

Out of the Heart of Man, Come Evil Thoughts 149

MUSTARD SEED   150

A Faith As a Grain of Mustard Seed 150
A Little Faith As a Grain of Mustard Seed 150

NEIGHBOR   151

You Shall Love Your Neighbor As You Love
    Yourself 151
The First and the Second Commandment 152

OVERCOME   152

In the World You Have Tribulation 152

PEACEMAKERS   153

Blessed Are the Peacemakers 153

PERFECT   153

If You Would Be Perfect, Go, Sell What You Possess
    and Give to the Poor 153

THE TEACHINGS OF JESUS

    You Must Be Perfect, As Your Heavenly Father Is Perfect 154

PERSECUTE   155

    Blessed Are Those Who Are Persecuted for Righteousness' Sake 155
    Blessed Are You When Men Revile You and Persecute You on My Account 155
    The Hour Is Coming When Whoever Kills You Will Think He Is Offering Service to God 156
    If They Persecuted Me, They Will Persecute You 156
    Your Reward Is Great in Heaven, for So Men Persecuted the Prophets Who Were Before You 156

PIETY   157

    When You Give Alms, Do Not Let Your Left Hand Know What Your Right Hand Is Doing 157

POOR   157

    When You Give a Feast, Invite the Poor, the Maimed, the Lame, the Blind 157

POOR IN SPIRIT   158

    Blessed Are the Poor in Spirit 158

POWER   158

    You Will See the Son of Man Seated at the Right Hand of Power, and Coming on the Clouds of Heaven 158

POWER OF CHRIST   159

    My Power Is Made Perfect in Weakness 159

I Perceive That Power Has Gone Forth from Me   159
For with Authority and Power He Commands the Unclean Spirits?   160
All the Crowd Sought To Touch Him, for Power Came Forth from Him and Healed Them All   161
They Will See the Son of Man Coming on the Clouds of Heaven with Power and Great Glory   161
Power and Authority over All Demons   162

PRAY   162

Always to Pray and Not Lose Heart   162
Watch and Pray That You May Not Enter into Temptation   163
This Kind Cannot Be Driven Out by Anything but Prayer   163
When You Pray, You Must Not Be Like the Hypocrites   164
Our Father   164
Watch at All Times, Praying That You May Have Strength to Escape All These Things   165

PRIDE   162

Out of the Heart of Man, Come Evil Thoughts   165

PROCLAIM   166

Leave the Dead to Bury Their Own Dead, but You Go and Proclaim the Kingdom of God   166

PROPHETS   167

Take Heed That No One Leads You Astray   167
Beware of False Prophets   168

Whatever You Wish That Men Would Do to You, Do
  So to Them   168
All the Prophets and the Law Prophesied Until John   168
I Have Come Not to Abolish the Law and the Prophets
  169
On the First and Second Commandment Depend All the
  Law and the Prophets   169
Woe to You, When All Men Speak Well of You   170

PURE IN HEART   **170**

Blessed Are the Pure in Heart   170

RAISE UP   **170**

I Will Raise Him Up at the Last Day   170
He Who Eats My Flesh and Drinks My Blood I Will
  Raise Him Up at the Last Day   171

READY   **171**

You Also Must Be Ready   171

REBUKE   **172**

If Your Brother Sins, Rebuke Him, and If He Repents,
  Forgive Him   172

RECEIVE   **172**

It Is More Blessed to Give   172

RECONCILED   **172**

First Be Reconciled to Your Brother, and Then Come
  and Offer Your Gift   172

RENOUNCE — 173

Whoever of You Does Not Renounce All That He Has Cannot Be My Disciple   173

If You Would Be Perfect, Go, Sell What You Possess and Give to the Poor   174

REPENT — 175

Joy in Heaven over One Sinner Who Repents   175

Woe to You, Chorazin, Bethsaida and Capernaum   175

If Your Brother Sins, Rebuke Him, and if He Repents, Forgive Him   176

Unless You Repent You Will All Likewise Perish   176

I Came Not to Call the Righteous, but Sinners   177

Repent, for the Kingdom of Heaven Is at Hand   177

RESIST — 177

Do Not Resist One Who Is Evil   177

REST — 178

You Will Find Rest for Your Souls   178

RESURRECTION — 178

I Am the Resurrection and the Life   178

RESURRECTION OF LIFE — 178

Those Who Have Done Good, Come Forth to the Resurrection of Life   178

RETURN — 179

What Shall a Man Give in Return for His Life   179

REVEALED — 179
Nothing Is Covered That Will Not Be Revealed 179

REVILE — 179
Blessed Are You When Men Revile You 179

REWARD — 180
Your Father Who Sees in Secret Will Reward You 180
Every One Who Has Left All, for My Name's Sake, Will Receive a Hundredfold, and Inherit Eternal Life 180

RICH MAN — 181
Woe to You That Are Rich 181
It Will Be Hard for a Rich Man to Enter the Kingdom of Heaven 181

RIGHTEOUS — 182
I Came Not to Call the Righteous, but Sinners 182
Seek First the Kingdom of God and His Righteousness 182
The Counselor Will Convince the World Concerning Sin and Righteousnes and Judgment 183
Blessed Are Those Who Hunger and Thirst for Righteousness 184
Blessed Are Those Who Are Persecuted for Righteousness' Sake 184
Your Righteousness Must Exceed That of the Scribes and Pharisees 185

RULER OF THIS WORLD — 185
Now Shall the Ruler of This World Be Cast Out 185

The Ruler of This World Is Judged   186

SABBATH   **186**

   Loosing from Satan's Bond on the Sabbath Day   186
   The Son of Man Is Lord Even of the Sabbath   187

SACRIFICE   **187**

   Go and Learn What This Means, `I Desire Mercy, and
      Not Sacrifice`   187
   I Desire Mercy, and Not Sacrifice   188

SALT   **188**

   You Are the Salt of the Earth   188

SATAN   **189**

   The Ruler of This World Is Judged   189
      Now Shall the Ruler of This World Be Cast Out   189
   Jesus Loosed a Daughter of Abraham from Bond on the
      Sabbath Day   189
   Satan Fall from Heaven   190

SAVED   **190**

   He Who Believes and Is Baptized Will Be Saved   190
   Who Then Can Be Saved?   191
   Gaining Your Lives   191

SAVIOR   **191**

   I Did Not Come to Judge the World but to Save the
      World   191

SEEK   192

    Every One Who Asks Receives, and He Who Seeks Finds, and to Him Who Knocks It Will Be Opened   192
    Seek First the Kingdom of God and His Righteousness   192

SERPENTS   193

    Be Wise As Serpents and Innocent As Doves   193

SERVANT   194

    Must Be Last of All and a Servant   194
    A Servant Is Not Greater Than His Master   194
    Who Is Greatest Among You Shall Be Your Servant   195
    Unworthy Servants   195
    Whoever Would Be Great Among You Must Be Your Servant   195
    I Am Among You As One Who Serves   196

SHEEP   196

    Sheep in the Midst of Wolves   196

SIGNS   197

    These Signs Are Written That You May Believe That Jesus Is the Christ, the Son of God   197
    The Signs Will Accompany Those Who Believe   197

SIN   198

    If You Were Blind, You Would Have No Guilt   198
    Woe to the Man Who Causes One of These Little Ones Who Believe in Me to Sin   198

They Have Seen and Hated Both Me and My Father 199
They Have No Excuse for Their Sin 199

SINNERS 199

I Came Not to Call the Righteous, but Sinners 199
Be Merciful, Even As Your Father Is Merciful 200

SLANDER 200

Out of the Heart of Man Come Evil Thoughts 200

SLAVE 201

Whoever Would Be First Among You Must Be Your Slave 201

SON OF MAN 202

You Will See the Son of Man Seated at the Right Hand of Power, and Coming on the Clouds of Heaven 202
They Will See the Son of Man Coming on the Clouds of Heaven with Power and Great Glory 202

SONS OF LIGHT 203

Believe in the Light, That You May Become Sons of Light 203

SPARROWS 203

You Are of More Value Than Many Sparrows 203

SPECK 204

You Hypocrite, First Take the Log Out of Your Own Eye 204

SPIRIT 204

Blessed Are the Poor in Spirit 204
THE SPIRIT INDEED IS WILLING, BUT THE FLESH IS WEAK 205
The Spirit Gives Life 205

SPIRIT DUMB AND DEAF 205

This Kind Cannot Be Driven Out by Anything but
  Prayer 205

SPIRIT OF GOD 206

Jesus Casts Out Demons by the Spirit of God 206

SPIRIT (HOLY SPIRIT) 206

Unless One Is Born of Water and the Spirit, He Cannot
  Enter the Kingdom of God 206
Whoever Blasphemes Against the Holy Spirit Never Has
  Forgiveness 206

STEAL 207

You Shall Not Steal 207

SWEAR 208

Do Not Swear at All 208

SWORD 208

All Who Take the Sword Will Perish by the Sword 208
I Have Not Come to Bring Peace, but a Sword 208

TAX COLLECTOR 209

If Your Brother Refuses to Listen Let Him Be to You
  As a Gentile and a Tax Collector 209

TEACHER 209

    You Call Me Teacher and Lord 209
    A Disciple Is Not Above His Teacher 210
    You Have One Teacher, the Christ 210

TEMPTATION 211

    Watch and Pray That You May Not Enter into Temptation 211
    Woe to the World for Temptations to Sin! 211
    Woe to the Man Who Causes One of These Little Ones Who Believe in Me to Sin 211

TESTIMONY 212

    We Speak of What We Know, and Bear Witness to What We Have Seen 212

THEFT 212

    Out of the Heart of Man, Come Evil Thoughts 212

THIRST 213

    Blessed Are Those Who Hunger and Thirst for Righteousness 213

TOMBS 214

    All Who Are in the Tombs Will Hear His Voice 214

TRADITION 214

    This People Honors Me with Their Lips, but Their Heart Is Far from Me 214

TREASURE 215

    Where Your Treasure Is, There Will Your Heart Be Also 215

TRESPASSES 215

    Forgive, That Your Father Also Who Is in Heaven May Forgive You Your Trespasses 215

    If You Do Not Forgive Men Their Trespasses, Neither Will Your Father Forgive Your Trespasses 216

TRIBULATION 216

    In the World You Have Tribulation 216

TROUBLE 216

    Let the Day's Own Trouble Be Sufficient for the Day 216

TRUTH 217

    If You Continue in My Word, You Will Know the Truth 217

UNCHASTITY 218

    Whoever Divorces His Wife, Except for Unchastity, and Marries Another, Commits Adultery 218

VICTOR 219

    I Have Overcome the World 219

VINE 220

    The Branch Cannot Bear Fruit by Itself, Unless It Abides in the Vine 220

Apart from Me You Can Do Nothing 220

WATCH AT ALL TIMES 220

Watch at All Times, Praying to Escape All That Will Take Place 220
The Son of Man Is Coming at an Hour You Do Not Expect 221
Watch and Pray 221
You Also Must Be Ready for the Son of Man Is Coming at an Unexpected Hour 221

WICKEDNESS 222

Out of the Heart of Man, Come Evil Thoughts 222

WITNESS 223

You Shall Not Bear False Witness 223

WOLVES 224

Sheep in the Midst of Wolves 224

WORD OF GOD 224

The Seed Is the Word of God 224
Man Shall Not Live by Bread Alone, but by Every Word That Proceeds from the Mouth of God 225

WORD OF JESUS 225

If any One Keeps My Word, He Will Never See Death 225
He Who Hears My Word and Believes Him Who Sent Me, Has Eternal Life 226
If You Continue in My Word, You Will Know the Truth 226

WORLD 226

    What Will It Profit a Man, if He Gains the Whole World and Forfeits His Life? 226
    You Shall Worship the Lord Your God and Him Only Shall You Serve 227
    Because You Are Not of the World, Therefore the World Hates You 227
    I Have Overcome the World 228

YOKE 228

    My Yoke Is Easy, and My Burden Is Light 228

www.ingramcontent.com/pod-product-compliance
Lightning Source LLC
Chambersburg PA
CBHW071653090426
42738CB00009B/1512